# THE BULLY STATE
## The End of Tolerance

# Brian Monteith

ISBN 978-0-9563720-0-0

Printed in Great Britain by the
MPG Books Group,
Bodmin and King's Lynn

Cover design by Dan Donovan
www.battenburg.biz

Typeset by Andrew Hook

Published by
The Free Society
Sheraton House
Castle Park
Cambridge CB3 0AX

www.thefreesociety.org

# About the author

Brian Monteith is an international communications consultant, writer and former member of the Scottish parliament where his colourful and forthright opinions upset his colleagues as often as they did his opponents.

A regular commentator in the Scottish media, Monteith can often be seen with a pint of ale in one hand, a mutton pie in the other, and a cigar in his mouth, but he is never lost for words defending peoples' right to live life the way they want to.

As founding president of the Parliamentary Pie Club, a member of Edinburgh's exclusive Cigar, Oyster and Tuesday clubs, and now driving his second Jaguar, Monteith has smoked, drank, eaten and driven for Britain.

In his first book, *Paying the Piper*, he argued why and how the state should get off people's backs so they can pay considerably less tax. Now his sights are on the nannies and the bullies who make life risk-free, joyless, bland and boring.

# Acknowledgements

This book would not have been possible without the encouragement and patience of Simon Clark, director of Forest (Freedom Organisation for the Right to Enjoy Smoking Tobacco). I make no apologies for a accepting the help of a smokers' rights group. I enjoy my cigars and like nothing better than an evening sitting with friends smoking a Partagas 'P series' No 2, while sipping a fine Scottish malt or supping a roasted malt stout, so why not defend the right of myself and others to enjoy this pastime as long as it is conducted in a civilised and well-mannered way? I only ask that others might show towards me the same good grace and tolerance that I show to those who choose to eat, drink and smoke what I might personally disapprove of.

While Simon made the book possible others came to my aid with ideas, anecdotes and stories including Graeme Brown, Iain Catto, Michael Fry and others in the Tuesday Club, Scotland's finest political dining club.

The books of Eamonn Butler (*The Rotten State of Britain*) and the late, great Ralph Harris (*Murder a Cigarette*, co-authored with Judith Hatton) were of special help and inspiration and I recommend them as further reading. I also suggest *Strictly No* by Simon Hills, *Scared to Death* by Christopher Booker and Richard North and *Nanny State: How food fascists, teetotalling do-gooders, priggish moralists, and other boneheaded bureaucrats are turning America into a nation of children* by David Harsani.

Likewise Google alerts, thefreesociety.org, taxpayersalliance.com, adamsmith.org and nannyknowsbest.blogspot.com were a regular source of information or leads that I could research further.

I should also thank the cities of Abuja, Berlin, Copenhagen, Edinburgh, New York, Paris, Port of Spain, Rome, Seattle and others that have revealed to me their different ways of treating drinkers, smokers and gourmands like me – and the various organisations that have inadvertently helped me visit them, most importantly Adam Smith International and the English Speaking Union. My views are of course my own and not theirs. I also wish to thank Luigi Capobianchi and his staff at Villa Milani, in Spoleto, Italy, where I found the necessary solace to complete the book without email or texts to disturb me.

Finally I would like to thank Jackie Lockett for reading my proofs and urging me to finish what was meant to be a short project but which took on a life of its own, such are the number of restrictions being introduced almost daily to police us.

Brian Monteith
September 2009

# CONTENTS

# Introduction

# NANNY IS NO LONGER ENOUGH

*"Even if I am a minority of one, truth is still the truth."*

\- MAHATMA GANDHI

Everyone has heard of the nanny state. Many objected to its pervasive influence in our daily lives, some reluctantly concluded that nanny really had our best interests at heart, while others worked feverishly to extend nanny's influence.

That was then, this is now. Nanny is no more. She has been dismissed, sent packing, told she is behind the times. A bright, brash, young thing has replaced benign old nanny. The bully is tough, malevolent and unrelenting in the pursuit of total control.

The state is no longer content to allow people their hard-fought liberties while pointing out the choices it would like us to make. Today the state goes to great lengths to not only direct or restrict our choices but to enter into our private domain. Our homes are no longer our castles as the state seeks to control our behaviour with intimidation and threats backed up by brute force. George Orwell's *Nineteen Eighty-Four* was a warning but it has become the apocryphal instruction manual.

Politicians seem to believe that while people are capable of electing their governments they are incapable of choosing when and how to eat, drink or smoke what's good (or bad) for them. Frankly, it's the politicians who are bad for us, not my steak tartare, my cigar or my large malt whisky. One of the regrettable consequences of the welfare state that was ushered in after the Second World War was the insidious belief that people no longer had responsibility for their own actions. The state would see you right, from cradle to grave. In fact, since the introduction of a benefit for unborn babies introduced by Gordon Brown in April 2009 the welfare state can officially be said to exist from womb to tomb.[1]

A sadly typical example of this corrosive effect on individual responsibility was reported in June 2005 when the mother of three girls, each of whom had a baby at the ages of 12, 14 or 16 respectively, blamed the state for its failure in teaching sex education. How the various nannies that have been calling for introducing school-based sex education at a younger and younger age must have agreed. The 16-year-old had already had two miscarriages and an abortion before giving birth.[2] We need welfare but it's a welfare society we need not a welfare state. A welfare society where individuals including parents accept responsibility for their actions (or lack of them) and don't pass the buck on to the conveniently faceless state, thus creating an incentive for the state to become more and more involved in our lives, introducing restrictions or trying to alter the behaviour of everyone so that the costs of its welfarism can be shared across the board.

One thing that has, for me, always marked out the doomsayers, the obsessionists, the persecutors, the 'Little Hitlers' and the malevolent power grabbers is their complete absence of humour. On the other hand I tend to find that those wishing to defend diversity, variance, individuality, non-conformism and other types of free-living have a tolerance that allows them to laugh at themselves and with others. Humour is of course a great weapon in debunking myths, slaying spurious claims often founded on junk science and upsetting the earnest do-gooders who mostly do so much that is bad. Sadly much of this book leaves one crying into one's pint (real ale, of course) rather than laughing, such are the bizarre schemes that people dream up to control us.

Examples of bullying are now becoming a weekly (if not daily) occurrence. I know because for two years now I have been running a 'Google alert' monitoring instances of individuals being bullied by jobsworths, politicians and frustrated and unfulfilled would-be autocrats.

What is it about so many politicians that they feel they should place their grubby hands all over our freedoms? Why are they such liberty takers? Westminster can be as out of touch as any parliament. Take, for example, the time MPs discussed the control of untidy gardens. Is this what motivates politicians nowadays, the desire to force residents to cut their grass and trim their hedges? There are laws available to deal with a neighbour's rat-infested jungle or other anti-social behaviour. Do we really need more legislation? It doesn't stop with our gardens. It happens very slowly, so you don't notice it. One by one our liberties are infringed until we are living in a society so intrusive that we don't know how to begin to challenge it.

It's all for our own good of course. "Have you got your seat belt on, sir? No? Here's an on-the-spot fine." A couple of years later and the question becomes: "Do the passengers in the back have their seat belts on, sir? No? Here's another fine." Saying it's good for you is no excuse for these parental interventions. The nanny state developed because of the misplaced belief that we can't be left to make our own judgments because, occasionally, someone might make the 'wrong' call, like not wearing a seat belt. And yet the truth is that left to our own devices most adults, even children, tend to make the same decisions that nanny would force upon us.

Our current government sees it differently as it erodes the right to trial before a jury and seeks to confiscate the wealth of those who are 'suspected' of drugs crimes (as opposed to convicted of any). Britain's sense of justice that all subjects are equal before the law and are presumed innocent until proven guilty is now regularly under assault. The losers are not only innocent individuals who are always caught up in government inefficiency, but also the police officers whose relationship with the public deteriorates as a contemptuous public unjustly holds them responsible.

A typically insidious idea came out of Tony Blair's favourite think tank and it's called data matching.[3] This would allow government departments to share information with each other so that your tax, welfare records and passport information can be pulled together. Eventually your parking fines, health record, school reports and all the rest would be added. How do we know that the information won't be sold by corrupt officials or, more likely, lost? Imagine this information being linked with the vehicle registration computer in Swansea and we're just one short step away from *Nineteen Eighty-Four*. Never mind the compulsory identity card: it would be called a driving licence.

Being so unaccountable to individual electors, the European Union poses the biggest threat to liberty and the Nice Treaty offers one of many examples. Take article 191. It allows the EU to take powers "to lay down regulations governing political parties". These regulations can be decided by qualified majority voting. British political parties that do not conform to European regulations could be made illegal. Where does this law place peaceful parties such as the United Kingdom Independence Party or others that offend the European Union?

For good to defeat evil politicians must marshal arguments that convince the electorate, not simply ban opponents. There are of course grey areas and nannying will always provoke debate. That's because it is generally well intentioned and a surprising number of people do want to be told what to do. They like the security it gives them. They want to be nudged, they want to conform. But bullying is different. Bullying is when the government grows impatient with nanny's progress and opts for coercion through fines, criminal prosecution, legal entry and the confiscation of private property to deliver its latest set of targets.

We also have to recognise that such is the onslaught against our hard won freedoms that, although there are many things that we may not care for ourselves – cigarette smoke in bars, rolls of body fat cascading over hipsters or the sport of fishing – it is in our own interests to defend smokers, burger-munchers and anglers because the denial of their freedoms makes the loss of the freedoms we cherish far easier and far more likely. This is no coincidence. The people who have sought over the last 30 years to limit our personal behaviour in areas such as smoking, eating, driving, drinking and other lifestyle choices are well co-ordinated, regularly share their experiences, and often move across sectors from one campaign to another.

The lessons learned from anti-smoking campaigns in Australia, the United States, Ireland and the United Kingdom have been studied and presented at seminars worldwide to ensure that each new campaign is adapted for the next battle. With such lobbying often successful, the usual suspects, be they politicians, so-called experts, media commentators or just the busy-body storm troopers, move on to the next 'deserving' cause such as restricting the availability of alcohol, changing the recipes of our favourite foods or forcing us to carry identity cards with our own personal number.

I agree with Patrick McGoohan's character in *The Prisoner* when he said, "I will not be pushed, filed, stamped, indexed, briefed, debriefed, or numbered. I am not a number, I am a free man!" I enjoy a cigar maybe once a week, I cook my own chips in beef dripping, use raw eggs in steak tartare, prefer unpasteurised cheese (and ales) and I am a sucker for a large fry-up. These are all my own conscious choices and I intend to live life the way I want to and I don't believe it is selfish of me to do so, especially when there are many others who would gladly share these experiences with me. Nor do I see any reason why I should be limited to practising some of these delights within the confines of our own home.

But we are no longer safe from nanny, even at home. In fact the very idea of a nanny state where nanny, who of course knows best, attempts to shape our lives in our 'best' interests is long gone. The nanny state has been replaced by the bully state. Not only are new laws being passed restricting our actions, little room is left for common sense exemptions and cultural practices while whole armies of health police are being recruited (at our expense) to persecute landlords, customers and people going about their daily business.

In the name of fighting against the evil that is smoking, for example, the strategy is to deliberately denormalise this everyday activity and stigmatise the smoker so that buying a pack of 20 cigarettes is enough to make people feel like pariahs, and that's even before they light up. In Scotland, actors on stage or in a film studio playing Churchill, Sherlock Holmes or performing the opening scene of *Carmen*, cannot light a cigar, pipe or cigarette. Cab drivers have been prosecuted for smoking in their own cars during private use if it is later used as a "public" vehicle. The campaign of intimidation against smokers is quite frightening.

Where this campaign of denormalisation has gone with smoking so will it go with alcohol and 'unhealthy' foods. Already the Scottish Parliament has restricted the hours that off-licences can open in the morning without any evidence that it was necessary or would be of benefit. Extra taxes and additional laws are continually being demanded to limit what we can eat, drink and smoke, even in our own homes and on our own property. Even as I was writing this the British Medical Association, which led the campaign to ban smoking in all enclosed public places, was demanding that Britain should become the first country in the world to introduce a comprehensive ban on all alcohol advertising, sponsorship and promotions. The BMA want this to "include all sports and music sponsorship, adverts in all media and end 'happy hour' and 'two-for-one' promotions". Other measures include "minimum pricing, an increase in taxation above the rate of inflation and to link the level to the alcoholic strength of the drink, reduce licensing hours in both off licences and pubs, and to force the drinks industry to pay for independent public health promotion".[4]

Transgressors are threatened with criminal records and when this is tied up with ideas such as identity cards the extent to which our lives will be monitored and ultimately controlled increases exponentially. We must therefore fight fire with fire. We must identify the links between the different bans and restrictions and support those whose habits we may not necessarily like or indulge in ourselves. If we don't our own lifestyles will be at risk.

It was this move from nannying, which I found irksome but was prepared to tolerate, towards outright bullying – the name calling, the prosecutions, the use of technology to control people's behaviour – that moved me to write this book. Once started the problem has been trying to stop because the information highlighting the growth of the nanny state and its mutation into the bully state never stops. At times it has been hard to know what to miss out.

So this book is really only a snapshot, a glance at what has been happening in Britain, North America and elsewhere over the last five years or so. If it can help raise awareness of the new threat to our liberties – not from a Soviet army flooding across the old Iron Curtain, not from our democracy falling to some autocrats of the so-called right or left, nor from old style socialism where the state owned everything but left us free to down a pint and smoke a fag at the bingo or the local club, but from the insidious creep of lifestyle control that extends into our homes, our cars and our social gatherings – then I shall be happy. And if you don't agree with what I've written, please recycle it. I wouldn't want the trees to have been used in vain.

Notes:
1. *Daily Mail*, 6 December 2006. In his tenth Pre-Budget Report, Gordon Brown said that women would receive payments from week 29 of pregnancy from April 2009
2. *Evening News*, Edinburgh, 17 June 2005
3. *Institute of Public Policy Research*
4. *Daily Telegraph*, 10 September 2009

# Chapter One

# THERE HAS ALWAYS BEEN A NANNY

*"The urge to save humanity is almost always*
*a false front for the urge to rule it."*

\- HENRY LOUIS MENCKEN

There has always been nanny, and there has always been the nanny state. Just as Maya, the wet nurse of the future pharaoh Tutankhamen, was honoured with her own tomb[1], a rarity for ordinary women in ancient times, we know that the classical state of Sparta forcibly removed its boys from their mothers at the age of seven to train them for military service.

It should be of no surprise that the noun 'nanny' should come to mean a caring protective outlook, especially when in the past so many rulers were likely to have had a nanny themselves. Nurses, wet nurses and nannies, not to be confused with governesses[2], were often given special privileges not reserved for other servants by the parents they helped, and might be expected to enjoy great affection from the children they reared. Among the British aristocracy nanny was often an influential figure who would be cared for by the family right through to her dotage. Mrs Everest, Winston Churchill's nanny, was held to have made a lasting impression on him.

Nanny, nurse or nursie can be found in literature such as Shakespeare's *Romeo and Juliet*, although none is more famous than Mary Poppins, the Edwardian nanny with magical powers who appeared in a series of books by P L Travers and was played by Julie Andrews in the famous Walt Disney film. In J M Barrie's *Peter Pan*, Nana the Newfoundland dog performs the task of nanny and in the real life story of Pu Yi, the last Chinese emperor, the wet nurse suckles the young prince right through his childhood.

Nannies are still prevalent today, although wet nursing is rare. Instead nannying is usually seen as a way for young girls to enjoy international travel. Britons still go abroad to widen their horizons while foreigners arrive in Britain and America to improve their English. The description was interchangeable with nurse but nanny is more common now.[3] The uniform has usually gone and the jobs tend to be shorter term and more mobile with a few men now in the role, leading to the horrible derivation of 'manny'.

Famous stories of real nannies make for interesting reading and are often more surprising than fiction might devise. For those wanting a treasure trove of the real world of nannies I cannot recommend highly enough Charlotte Zeepvat's book *From Cradle to Crown: British Nannies and Governesses at the World's Royal Courts* (unfortunately, now out of print). [4] Delving into the lives of some 120 British nannies who worked for royalty from the 1770s to the 1950s, Zeepvat reveals the enchanting, influential, warm and loyal lives of so many women in a time when men were all powerful.

She tells of the unknown and the famous such as Kitty Strutton, a bricklayer's daughter from Hackney who, when she died in St Petersburg, was honoured by the Tsar of Russia and his four brothers walking through the snow behind her coffin. Or Frances Fry who saved the life of her premature charge Grand Duke Dmitri Pavlovich, a man who grew up to become one of the murderers of Rasputin. Other famous nannies included Margaret Eagar, from County Limerick, who was the nanny to Olga, Tatiana, Maria and Anastasia Romanov, the four daughters of the last Tsar of Russia,

Nicholas II. Her indelible contribution to the Grand Duchesses was to leave them with an Irish brogue when they spoke English, something that elocution lessons were required to deal with! Better known still was Charlotte Bill, known as "Lalla", who raised the children of the Duke and Duchess of York, later to become King George V and Queen Mary, including Prince John who died in 1919 from a severe epileptic fit at the age of 13.

Nannies have often captured the imagination of dramatists, not least because the audience is more able to empathise with a nurse's perspective than that of her aristocratic employers while allowing entry into a world of stately homes, power intrigues, human failings and historical events. Prince John and Lalla Bill were the subject of an Emmy award-winning drama by Stephen Poliakoff for the BBC entitled *The Lost Prince*.

Being so close to the private lives of the great and the good made nannies particularly attractive to publishers. Marion Crawford, governess and nanny to the princesses Elizabeth and Margaret Rose of York and dubbed 'Crawfie' by Margaret, became especially controversial when she became the first royal servant to sell her story for financial reward. Following the abdication of their uncle, King Edward VIII, Elizabeth was heiress presumptive and Crawfie remained in the service of both princesses until Elizabeth married HRH the Duke of Edinburgh when she was 21 in 1947.

When Crawfie published her memoirs she was banished from the Royal Court and neither of her charges ever spoke to her again. Although she had thought that her contract with the publishers would require any articles to be cleared by the Royal Family (her publishers had been advised by the government of the day to approach her for some helpful public relations stories), she had been duped and publication went ahead regardless in the UK and USA. The articles were developed into a book, *The Little Princesses: The Story of the Queen's Childhood by her Nanny*, for which Crawford received $85,000.[5]

In recent times the most well-known nanny was arguably Tiggy

Legge-Bourke, nanny to Prince William and Prince Harry, who due to the circumstances surrounding the break-up of the Prince of Wales' marriage and the gossip spread about her by the Princess of Wales became a minor media celebrity in the early Nineties. More recently the skills required to control difficult or unruly children have been promoted on television by Jo Frost, the self-styled 'Supernanny', whose modus operandi is based on common sense laced with a heavy dose of patience, which is edited out of the show for the viewers' benefit. A child standing on a naughty step for 30 minutes doesn't make good television.

Such a maternalistic institution, even though it was on the wane by the 1950s, was bound to be held in affection by those who experienced, came into contact with or read about it. The cultural conceit that nanny was sure to look after one's best interests was for most British people taken in with their mother's milk, or even their wet nurses'. It was therefore all too easy for 'nanny' to become a metaphor for the state as it tried to protect its people, either for their 'own good' or because the state had a vested interest in shaping their behaviour.

The first recorded use of the term 'nanny state' is credited to Conservative politician Iain Macleod, one-time editor of *The Spectator*. Writing in the magazine on 3 December 1965 Macleod referred to "what I like to call the nanny state". Whether by accident or design, it was an association that was to stick with him. Macleod, described by the Marquess of Salisbury as "too clever by half", had a knack of coming up with memorable phrases. He was also credited with coining the phrase "stagflation".[6] Ironically, given the nature of what was yet to come, Macleod was the politician who in 1952 made the announcement that British clinician Richard Doll had established a link between smoking tobacco and lung cancer. (Macleod reputedly chain-smoked throughout the press conference.)

On 20 June 1970 Macleod became Edward Heath's first chancellor of the exchequer but was in the job for only one month before he died from a severe heart attack on 20 July. He left a draft budget that included the abolition of free school milk to children of families not receiving benefit, a policy introduced infamously and credited to the then education secretary Margaret Thatcher even though she argued against it in cabinet. Whether Iain Mcleod saw free school milk as a cost cutting exercise or too much nannying is open to debate.

Rules and regulations that sought to shape the actions of the populace, whether by monarchies, theocracies or autocrats, has existed since the days of antiquity. The most notable are the rules that are still with us today about which foods to eat, how and when. Alcohol has always had rules governing its consumption, and 'acceptable' sexual practices vary from authority to authority, even if those who regulate them practice something quite different in private.

So what is a nanny state or, more particularly, what are the policies that create such a society? Nannying comes in many forms but includes government intervention – supra-national, national or local – and the intervention of professional bodies that have gained the status of authority and whose own codes dictate how services shall be delivered. Such interventions are designed to shape our lifestyle or behaviour and they include but are not limited to the introduction of laws, the restriction of choice, and punitive taxation.

In many cases there is an assumption that without intervention the individual or group being 'protected' will make the 'wrong' choice. Wrong for whom? Often the government wants to minimise its costs in, say, the NHS even though, in the case of smokers, the taxpayer would be better off if people carried on smoking, paying their tobacco taxes and receiving less pension funds because they might be expected to have a shorter lifespan.

Libertarians or real liberals (that is, classical liberals) often argue against nanny state interventions for two simple reasons: one, people should be free to make their own choices so long as they do not impinge on the liberties of others; and, two, they should not be protected from making bad choices because it's important that individuals and others learn from the consequences of their actions.

There are academics and polemicists such as Noam Chomsky who argue that some forms of national economic intervention are akin to the nanny state looking after government-favoured industries, be they state or private, although I suspect it is an intentionally ironic metaphor rather than a widely accepted or understood usage. It may serve to make a point, although I'm not sure everyone would 'get it'. Personally I think it rather devalues and confuses the real meaning and I would urge those fighting the nanny state to keep it simple and keep it focused. To borrow a phrase from self help guru Stephen J Covey, "The main thing is to keep the main thing the main thing".

Similarly some liberals, in the corrupted sense of the word, argue that there is a conservative nanny state, one that protects certain social practices, businesses or an elite, working against the wider public interest. This is an argument I am perfectly willing to accept in principle, although I might disagree over the detail.

During my time in the Conservative party I've come across many individuals who have had their own pet schemes to nanny people, although they have usually stemmed from a resistance to change, such as the desire to ban supermarkets in order to protect smaller local shops, or some particular moral code that leads to the censorship of, for example, computer games or videos and DVDs. Rarely have I met a conservative who wants to 'nanny' the business classes, or those with new money or old. Still, the Tory party remains a broad church and I'm sure there are a few under some stone or other. The majority of this book will concentrate on the generally understood use of the term. That is, the attempt by the state, its agents or unaccountable bodies supported by the state, to shape our lives. Having reviewed the extent to which the nanny state has grown, I shall then consider how the nanny state is evolving into a far nastier bully state, seeking to coerce and criminalise people who will not take the hint.

While nannies and the nanny state have in their various guises always been with us, the modern beginnings of the nanny state in Britain began with the social reforms of the Victorian era and the interventions made to protect public health. For me this was not nannying as such, as I shall try to explain, but it did create a professional class of people who later, having exhausted their role, found justification for interventions that would previously have been thought excessive.

Public health has come a long way since it was primarily concerned with preventing contagious and infectious diseases, threats to health that individuals could not necessarily prevent and whereby the group, in this case the public, required protection. In many cases treating a disease is not just important for the sick individual but can be vital to prevent its spread to others.

Public health programmes in areas of infection and contagion, such as smallpox where vaccinations can be used, have had a major effect in its eradication, even though it was the scourge of humankind for thousands of years. The great engineering works of the nineteenth century that sought to ensure clean water and the removal of effluent from urban development, be they initially founded on the miasma theory or its replacement, germ theory, were clearly a public good that delivered significant improvements to public health. The problems could be identified, measured and the outcomes assessed. Faced with smallpox or cholera few, if any, would oppose vaccination or clean water and sanitation.

Public health stepped over the line of tackling infection and contagion, however, when, in 1920 C E A Winslow defined public health as "the science and art of preventing disease, prolonging life and promoting health through the organized efforts and informed choices of society, organizations, public and private, communities and individuals".[7] That was a rather sweeping, all-inclusive justification for all sorts of measures and it shouldn't surprise anyone that such a large public health industry has since grown up, bossing us about and "prolonging life" through "organised efforts".

7

If public health is to be concerned about the overall well being of society then it must in the end seek to intervene to show that its investment has brought some measureable improvement. When the answer to polio or an identifiable strain of flu is mass vaccination one can see the point of public health. When it is used to combat what are seen to be poor personal choices by adults, such as too much alcohol, too little exercise or smoking any amount of tobacco, public health programmes will inevitably clash with individual liberty. Nobody wishes to contract polio or catch a virulent flu, but millions do wish to share a bottle of wine every night with their partner, taking them well beyond the recommended weekly intake of alcohol units. As a result public health is undoubtedly a contributor to the nanny state mentality of modern times. Having largely conquered the diseases that wreaked havoc in the nineteenth and much of the twentieth centuries, such as cholera, typhoid and tuberculosis, public health has turned its attention to illnesses that are more prone in older age and might reflect personal behaviour from adulthood onwards.

The way that public health is governed varies from country to country. Some health authorities are centralised, some are devolved, and this is often reflected in the application of laws and regulations. In the United States, for example, one finds that the laws governing alcohol consumption, smoking and road safety differ from state to state. In other countries – Spain, for example – the same laws are introduced across the whole country, whereas in Britain regulations can be introduced nationally or ceded to regional parliaments or assemblies or even local authorities. What is certain is that there is an international network of public health bodies and through their conferences, seminars and academic meetings they share information that encourages a rising level of nanny state interventionism. What has worked 'successfully' in Australia or Canada to denormalise smoking, for example, will be recommended to activists in Britain and elsewhere. I recall, for instance, seeing cigarette packets with photographs of blackened lungs when I was in Toronto in 2001 and I knew immediately that it would only be a matter of time before the same idea was introduced in Britain.

Public health today is more attracted to involve itself in issues surrounding population growth and the politics and economics of poverty (because wealth or the lack of it can effect health), education (because ignorance can effect health) and inequality (because that covers all the other bases!). The result can be seen whereby unelected and unaccountable taxpayer funded bodies like the Tayside Health Board in Scotland thinks it has a role campaigning for legislative changes to restrict alcohol sales to adults, adults old enough to die fighting for their country in Iraq. Indeed politicians who dare to resist the constant clamour for further health protection and ever larger budgets will find themselves assailed by all sorts of 'experts' and authorities who never have to raise taxes or face the electorate.

The media is similarly assaulted by a steady stream of news releases, PR stunts, giveaways and junk science dressed up as authoritative research from quangos and politically-active charities that have morphed into lobby groups. Hardly a day goes by when we aren't being told to stop drinking coffee or start eating oily fish. Then it's start drinking coffee and don't bother with oily fish. Talk about mixed messages! The latest 'do this, do that' is aspirin which until recently was being flagged up as an aid to ward off strokes because it thins the blood. Suddenly we're being told that it's a health risk to some and of no valuable effect generally.

The constant lobbying and campaigning by government departments and agencies (often dressed up as 'charities') creates a toxic, febrile atmosphere far more injurious to the health of the nation than many of the causes they campaign on. Their actions are certainly harmful to serious and objective evidence-based discussion. (The smoking ban is a case in point because it was only after MPs had voted for a comprehensive public smoking ban that the House of Lords Economic Affairs Committee heard extensive evidence and concluded that the ban was disproportionate to the risks of so-called passive smoking. By then of course it was too late.

If only MPs had listened to the same evidence with the same level of impartiality. Unfortunately most MPs only had ears for the powerful anti-smoking lobby.)

I decided long ago to eat and drink what I liked but to vary it as often as possible and consume it in moderation, a path that I admit I occasionally stray from. Nevertheless, as the former president of the Parliamentary Pie Club at the Scottish Parliament I wasn't surprised when even the humble mutton pie was attacked by food fascists as a danger to my health. But how many people eat a mutton pie every day of their lives? It's the same with McDonald's or other fast food outlets. As far as I can tell, the alleged danger is based on the idea that you go to these restaurants every day and gorge yourself on the largest meals possible. Most people just don't live that way.

Unfortunately, having tackled the real and identifiable publicly transmitted threats to our well being, the public health industry had to find some way to maintain and develop its status. By expressing concern about health inequalities caused by, say, unemployment or housing, the public health industry has ensured that the gravy train of jobs, budgets, conferences and training continues to grow. Meanwhile the poor remain poor and the homeless continue to look for shelter, in many parts of Britain actually growing in number. Public health campaigns in areas of choice or behaviour have more debatable effects, often because the evidence they are based upon, such as the effects of secondhand smoke, is highly debatable.

In human behaviour there is also the problem of unintended consequences whereby people react in unanticipated ways. One example of how concern for public health strayed into areas that are difficult to measure and have unforeseen outcomes was the decision to introduce compulsory seat belts in cars. Car manufacturers in the United States fitted front seat belt anchors voluntarily from 1962 while the first legal requirement to factory fit belts in cars appeared in the states of Victoria and South Australia in 1964. The UK followed suit in 1967. Various attempts to make the wearing of seat belts compulsory in the UK were subsequently tried but failed. In

1981, however, Lord Nugent, president of the Royal Society for the Prevention of Accidents (RoSPA), managed to amend the 1981 Transport Bill so that the compulsory wearing of seat belts was given a three-year trial. The trial began on 31 January 1983 and in 1986 parliament voted to keep the law. By 1991 it had become compulsory to wear seat belts in the back as well.[8]

The effects of wearing seat belts remain contested to this day. A study by Professor John Adams of University College London, published in 1982, concluded that 15 of the 18 countries surveyed with compulsory seat belt laws (amounting to 80 per cent of the world's motoring) had fared no better in fatalities and injuries, while New Zealand, Sweden and Ireland were significantly worse than those without the belts.[9] Adams didn't challenge the idea that seat belts protect people from the physical damage that can be sustained inside a car when it crashes. Indeed, he accepted the evidence of the many tests that had been conducted to show this. What he did develop was the theory that protecting drivers from the consequences of bad driving served to encourage bad driving, a factor known as risk compensation.

A number of studies into the behaviour of drivers in different conditions, including taxi drivers being asked by their passengers to belt up or not belt up on the same route, found that drivers wearing a seat belt drove faster and closer to the car in front. A Department of Transport report, known as the Isles Report after its author J E Isles, considered the evidence from a number of European countries that had compulsory seat belt laws and compared it with evidence from the UK and Italy where, at the time, the use of seat belts was not compulsory. The report predicted a 2.5 per cent increase in fatalities among those inside cars if seat belts were made compulsory in Britain. The report was suppressed and lay unpublished until after the House of Commons had voted to introduce the compulsory trial, when it was leaked to *The Spectator*. Isles found that in Europe the trend in countries with compulsory seat belt laws was for a growth in injuries to non-car users such as pedestrians and cyclists.

Compulsory seat belts were introduced in Britain at the same time as evidential roadside breath testing, thus ensuring that the use of statistics to measure the contribution that either law had made to a reduction in accidents and the saving of lives would be impossible. There followed a reduction in driver fatalities and injuries and an increase in non-car user fatalities and injuries. Rear passengers, who were not then covered by the law, suffered an increase in fatalities. The predicted saving, bandied about by politicians including the then secretary of state for transport William Rodgers, of 1,000 fatalities and 10,000 injuries per year did not materialise and in January 1986 *The Lancet* commented on the "unexplained and worrying increase in deaths of other road users".

In 1997 the Department of Transport and Roads reported that "since seat belt wearing was made compulsory in 1983 it has reduced casualties by at least 370 deaths and 7,000 serious injuries per year".[10] Given that there are many other factors to contend with (drink-drive laws and campaigns, more safety features, safer roads, better braking, more congestion slowing traffic down) the claim that compulsory seat belts have significantly reduced car crash fatalities and injuries that has not been offset by deaths and injuries for other road users and pedestrians is very difficult to prove.

In *The effects of seat belt legislation on road casualties in Great Britain* by J Durbin and A Harvey[11], an analysis of fatality figures before and after the law, commissioned by the Department of Transport, the evidence showed (a) a clear increase in pedestrian, cyclist and rear-passenger fatalities in collisions involving passenger cars; (b) no such increase in casualties in collisions involving buses and goods vehicles, which were exempt from the law; (c) a reduction in the number of drivers found to be drunk at the scene of collisions; (d) a reduction in overall fatalities between the hours of 20.00 and 04.00 (peak hours for drink-driving offences); and (e) no reduction in overall fatality rates outside these hours.

One of the complicating factors that makes compulsory wearing of seat belts so controversial is that it can result in the death of the person wearing them, from neck and spine injuries incurred by the restraining force in an accident, from those in the rear not being belted (and other loose but hard or heavy items) becoming projectiles, and from cardiac arrest caused by severe chest compressions. Examples of people surviving car crashes by being thrown clear are well documented. Indeed the famous German avant garde artist Joseph Beuys even survived his Ju 87 'Stuka' aircraft being shot down when, unstrapped, he was thrown clear into the snow on impact, while the strapped-in pilot perished.

Can it be right to force by law someone to strap themselves into a car when the evidence suggests that not only might it cause the death of the wearer in the result of a crash, but that it is also likely to make a crash more likely through an unconscious increase in risk taking or faster driving? Surely not wearing a seat belt is a victimless crime and drivers and passengers should be free to decide for themselves? If there is a case for the compulsory wearing of seatbelts should it not be restricted to rear seat passengers who can become unintended projectiles in the event of a crash? Even then one could argue that is a judgment for the driver to make. Many believe, and I agree with them even though I normally wear a seat belt myself, that government should not legislate for a law that might cost someone's life in the hope that it might save the lives of others.

In time, especially if not challenged, nanny state interventionism becomes the norm. Forcing motorcyclists to wear a crash helmet is another example. Introduced by the Conservatives in 1972 it was not a popular measure amongst bikers and was particularly resisted by Sikhs, a story I relate in the next chapter. Now, some 36 years later, compulsory crash helmets are seen as the default position. In the United States the situation varies from state to state. Some states have no laws for crash helmets and are also more relaxed about seat belts in cars.

It is time for people and politicians to wake up to the role of public health – and its younger sister, health and safety – in wrapping us up in cotton wool and bandages made of laws, regulation, targets, initiatives and all the retraining and reprogramming that goes with it. They are the progenitors of the modern nanny state. It is this nannying belief that our mortal fate can be delayed, almost indefinitely, when many of us, maybe most of us, would just like to enjoy our time while we are here, that frustrates so many people. In the past many of us have been willing to accept some degree of nannying but its incessant, inexorable growth is causing many now to resist, leading in its own way to nanny being given her jotters as she's no longer fit for purpose.

Unfortunately some politicians have taken this as a signal that it's time to resort to bullying where resistance will be punished and our lives will be controlled to the nth degree. They don't see it that way, of course. Instead politicians talk about "nudging" people to change their habits. The truth, as we all know, is that politicians and public health campaigners don't like it when people ignore them and as we will see in subsequent chapters, it's a small step from nudging to shameless bullying.

Notes:
1. *Daily Telegraph*, Sydney 4 June 2008
2. While they could double up as nannies, governesses had an educational role. The most famous governess is probably Anna Leonowens, who worked at the Royal Court of the King of Siam and became the subject of the film, *The King and I*, with Deborah Kerr and Yul Bryner in the lead roles.
3. The job should not be confused with child minder. A nanny works in the house of the employer; a child minder receives children to his or her own home, often having children from one or more families.
4. *From cradle to crown: British nannies and governesses at the world's royal courts*, Charlotte Zeepvat. Sutton Publishing. ISBN 0-7509-3074-8
5. *The Little Princesses: The Story of the Queen's Childhood by her Nanny*
6. House of Commons, 17th November 1965
7. Charles-Edward Amory Winslow, founder of Yale School of Public Health

8.  RoSPA History – How belting up became law, www.RoSPA.com
9.  Society of Automotive Engineers
10. *The Lancet*, 11 January 1986, p75
11. Durbin J, Harvey A: *The effects of seat belt legislation on road casualties in Great Britain*, Department of Transport, October 1985

# Chapter Two

# NANNY GAINS WEIGHT

*"They that can give up essential liberty to obtain a little temporary safety deserve neither liberty nor safety"*

- BENJAMIN FRANKLIN

Over the course of the twentieth century nanny grew and grew from a nimble size eight to a mature size eighteen, then ballooned to a size twenty-eight. From a mere slip of a thing nanny had become a matron as obese as any of those in her charge. One example of this continual growth was the slow but exponential invasiveness of health and safety as a means to control the population. Politicians increasingly use health and safety and its corollary, the threat of litigation for failing to take adequate precautions to protect workers, consumers or mere passers-by, as a handy excuse to back up their unhealthy desire for more control over our lives.

We should be careful however not to mistake the growth of public health in Europe, and the health and safety culture that germinated and blossomed in America and is now slowly engulfing the world like some parasitic vine, as the causes of our new bully state. They are not the reason for our pain. They are just two more cudgels that the new bullies use to beat us with. They are not causes but symptoms. It is politicians of all parties who are to blame. Taking legitimate concerns about poor hygiene and poor working conditions, or street pavements or ladders and such like, and using them as justification to use the force of law to dominate people's lives, is more about politicians justifying their existence or seeking greater power than paying due regard to how we might better protect ourselves by taking greater responsibility for our actions.

The urge to protect us from ourselves, as opposed to protecting us from each other, grew apace in the twentieth century. For instance, who would have thought in that as a direct consequence of the death in 1935 of T E Lawrence from head injuries, sustained when he lost control of his motorcycle and crashed, that every motorcyclist would be forced to wear a crash helmet? The young neurosurgeon Hugh Cairns, later to be knighted, was one of those attending to Lawrence and he was so affected that he went on to research such injuries and the need for protection. He campaigned successfully at the outset of the Second World War for the British Army to make protective helmets standard issue in order to save what he considered to be the unnecessary loss of soldiers' lives.[1]

In 1972 Section 32 of the new Road Traffic Act made it a legal requirement for all motorcyclists on public roads to wear protective headgear from 1 June 1973. The Bill was met with vociferous protests from bikers that were ultimately ignored. Particularly notable amongst the protestors was Yorkshireman Fred Hill, a former Second World War army dispatch rider who later became a mathematics teacher. He probably never anticipated just how much riding a motorcycle with his old beret on would throw him into the limelight.

Fred Hill took his protest around Britain, riding everywhere with his trademark beret instead of a crash helmet. It earned him hundreds of tickets that he refused to pay, keeping them all in a large suitcase. It was only a matter of time before he was judged to be in contempt of court and given a prison sentence. In the end he received no fewer than 31 jail sentences. Anecdotes about Fred are legion. Two charming stories of this man, who had put his life at risk in service for his country and in the name of freedom, involve a lady magistrate and a desk sergeant. The magistrate lectured him about his lawlessness, especially given that it was intentional, whereupon Fred replied that if it was not for members of her sex breaking the law some years before she would not be sitting on the bench in front of him. Some of Fred's sentences reflected a more tolerant understanding of his belief in freedom with one sentence as short as 24 hours. This resulted in his cell door being left open and the desk sergeant telling him to "Bugger-off when no-one's looking". Eventually the local police began to turn a blind eye to his protests, but as soon as he ventured further afield the suitcase had a few more tickets and summonses to accommodate.

Demonstrations against the law would often have Hill dressed in an arrow-patterned prison suit entertaining the crowd with his good humour and telling others to join him by refusing to wear a helmet. Fortunately he was never charged with the more serious crime of incitement to break the law! In every other respect Fred Hill was a law abiding citizen and it says everything about him and so much about the politicians who he felt had betrayed his freedom that he carried on protesting until 1984 when, at the age of 74, he died of a heart attack whilst in custody for a ridiculous 60 days in Pentonville Prison. He had been warned by the prison governor that the harsh prison environment could be the death of him, to which Fred relied nobly that it wasn't important where a man died but how. It was a warning he was prepared to ignore, and so it came to pass.

A tribute to Fred Hill is made every year at the gates of Pentonville by the Motorcycle Action Group (MAG), a body that he was a founder member of when it was established to campaign against the law, something it continues to do to this day. As Philip Neale says on the MAG website, "Motorcycling is about freedom. Fred understood that. We must never forget Fred's example lest we forget why we ride motorcycles".[2] Amen to that.

One concession granted was to allow followers of the Sikh faith the freedom not to wear a crash helmet as long as they were wearing a turban. Sikhs had been especially incensed by the introduction of the law, coming as it did a few years after they had won a famous ruling that allowed them to wear turbans while working on Wolverhampton Council buses, setting a precedent for others to follow. As a result some Sikhs deliberately flouted the law, riding around on motorcycles with their turbans on instead of crash helmets, and a court case appealing against the conviction of Baldev Singh Chalhal went all the way to the High Court. The Labour government eventually granted the exemption when it agreed to support a private member's bill, the Motor-Cycle Crash Helmets (Religious Exemption) Act (1976) introduced by the Southall MP Sidney Bidwell. It was reaffirmed by the Conservative government in the Road Traffic Act (1988).[3]

It is often said that if a motorcyclist is not wearing a crash helmet then he or she already has brain damage. Nevertheless, is it right to force bikers to wear a helmet? As with seat belts, there is no victim other than, potentially, the person choosing not to wear one. You may be foolish not to wear a crash helmet but when did it become a crime to be foolish?

Likewise it is argued that helmetless motorcyclists do have an impact on others in that the additional costs of attending to accidents and dealing with the aftermath of rehabilitating a crash survivor is born by the state – in other words, the taxpayer. To that I would argue two things. First, in the event of a motorcycle accident an ambulance and police are likely to be required at the scene irrespective of whether a helmet was worn. Second, why not allow a compromise whereby people would have the right to choose to wear a crash helmet or not, so long as they have insurance that would cover their health costs? This would remove the burden to the taxpayer that some people object to and negate the argument that one person's actions has a financial impact on everyone else.

Of course motorcyclists will say they are taxpayers too and the emergency services and the NHS have a duty to attend to and treat all accident victims. Anyway, why pick on motorcyclists for special treatment? Are stranded climbers or marooned sailors asked to pay for the hundreds of thousands of pounds that the taxpayer has to spend rescuing them or picking up the pieces?

With the compulsory crash helmet law introduced in Britain in 1973 it was only a matter of time (ten years to be exact) before the argument about protecting "stupid" people from themselves would be used to justify the compulsory wearing of seat belts in cars. And so it proved. No matter who was in power, Labour or Conservative, nanny kept on growing. For many politicians passing new laws to shape our behaviour is like injecting a particularly strong narcotic, providing some sort of addictive fix that must be taken at regular intervals otherwise they feel depressed, lifeless, unwanted, unloved and without purpose. The periodic elections, which they all say they enjoy, are just a glorified turf war to gain control of the racket that feeds their habit.

Admittedly some good things have come from new legislation, but most of the time it's from repealing old laws rather than inventing new ones. Repealing the Corn Laws ensured that more people had bread on the table, while repealing the various restrictions brought in during the First World War to control housing rents and alcohol sales resulted in more housing and relaxed moderate drinking for the vast majority. Nowadays, however, few people talk about repealing laws, however draconian they are (like the public smoking ban). Instead the newspapers are full of demands for yet more laws in the belief that human behaviour can be controlled or "nudged" in a particular direction.

The Scottish Parliament decided that owners of pubs and restaurants should face a criminal conviction and a £2,500 fine if they asked any woman to stop breast-feeding their little nipper on their premises. Breast-feeding is already far more widely accepted in public than it was ten or 20 years ago so why introduce a law when this voluntary, evolutionary process of change was already happening? Passing a law that makes criminals out of proprietors is ridiculous. Instead of respecting the freedom of publicans and café owners to run their establishments as they see fit, the supporters of this law wanted to step in and make them conform to their view of what is right. Such an attitude is not compatible with a free society. The simple fact is, if there is a demand for more places to cater for breastfeeding then new or existing establishments will change their policy to meet public demand. That's how the free market works. We don't need new laws to enforce policies that will happen in their own good time.

Meanwhile the UK parliament decided that a special law was necessary to prevent people using their mobile phones whilst driving. Don't get me wrong. I understand that to drive safely you should have both hands on the wheel. Research in both the UK and the United States suggests that using a mobile phone while driving is a potentially dangerous distraction. But did we really need new legislation? What was wrong with existing laws that were designed to combat dangerous driving or driving without due care and attention? Sometimes new laws appear to be introduced just for the sake of it and because they are so specific they allow no room for a common sense interpretation of the law that will take into account other factors – in this example road conditions, density of traffic and so on.

Some campaigners want to go further still and ban hands free telephones. What about all the other distractions that drivers face? Should we ban kids from quarrelling in the back seat, or dogs from jumping about? Changing a CD, eating, drinking, applying make-up or shouting at the infuriating Nicky Campbell on the radio can distract you too. Should there be specific laws to ban them as well?

In fact we already know what the next step is. Having banned smoking in company vehicles they now want to ban smoking in private cars despite the fact that there is no evidence that smoking while driving is a serious risk to anyone's safety. Initially the ban will be introduced to 'protect' children from the alleged effects of secondhand smoke. Within a few years, unless we stand our ground, I predict that smoking while driving will be banned completely, regardless of the presence of children or whether the vehicle is stationary or on the move. I'll take bets that if you are caught driving while smoking you'll get the same fine, plus three points on your licence, that you currently get for using a mobile phone.

The bottom line is we have far too many laws already and some of our good laws are perfectly adequate but are just not enforced. I'd far rather we gave more resources to the police and the courts to apply the laws we already have before we rush into creating new ones.

The Institution of Occupational Safety and Health (IOSH) blames 'rogue consultants' for the misunderstanding, misrepresentation and myths surrounding health and safety. The IOSH claims that the 'if in doubt ban it' brigade may not be 'qualified' members of the profession and are giving the industry a bad name. Apparently anyone can set themselves up as a health and safety adviser and the IOSH want regulations to prevent that. As Claire Fox, director of the Institute of Ideas, so brilliantly argued on The Free Society website in 2008: "It seems beyond parody that an organisation which stands accused of over regulating everyone else's lives should suggest tighter regulation of its own. The sector is littered with good practice guidelines and training courses, while the Health and Safety Executive has issued a set of key principles emphasising the need to balance benefits and risks. Common sense has not and cannot prevail because this whole approach misses the point – people have to take more responsibility for their actions."

The sly way that the public smoking ban was introduced in Ireland and then Scotland is a clear example of health and safety being used as a weapon by the nanny state. Its advocates in the Dail and Holyrood parliaments went to great lengths to talk about how the smoking ban would "protect" bar workers and spurious statistics were flaunted regularly to justify such punitive interventionism. Yet one did not have to scratch too hard to find that the real goal wasn't the protection of bar workers (there was very little evidence to suggest that staff were at serious risk from secondhand smoke) but the Orwellian 'denormalisation' of smoking.

In seminars and conferences held subsequently to explain how the Scottish ban was introduced, how 'successful' it had been and what measures might be planned next, it was clear that the public message was health and safety but the political imperative was denormalisation, reducing smokers to the role of social pariahs. Written evidence in submissions and reports backed this up. The claim was made, unsubstantiated by any meaningful evidence, that bar staff had never been healthier, a rather spurious claim given that a great many bar staff smoke and many were losing their jobs as the licensed trade contracted following the introduction of the ban.

The growth of the nanny state was not just in how she intruded into our lives but also how she was given a new, louder voice, more like a megaphone. The increase in public health advertising and other government 'information' campaigns has been phenomenal. What is the point of these campaigns? You see them incessantly on television and they dominate the 48-sheet hoardings that brighten up our bleakest urban landscapes. But do they have any tangible benefit and are there better alternatives? It's a question worth asking because, as in other areas, the attitude among politicians is to spend even more of our money, regardless of the result.

One of the more expensive initiatives was the Scottish Executive's 2003 Healthy Living campaign, launched in a country that is consistently at the wrong end of all the ill-health league tables. At first it generated a lively response in the number of calls to the campaign helpline but these quickly fell off. With so few calls the cost of handling them was transferred to the NHS 24-hour helpline. For the Executive this had the benefit of making it impossible for its critics to break down the unit cost of each call. The public's requests for healthy living advice initially seemed to correlate with the volume of advertising, but a year later an increase in advertising spend failed to produce a significant rise in the number of calls. The result of the Healthy Living campaign now look pretty ugly and no amount of cosmetic surgery can make the figures look pretty.

Government ministers, both at Holyrood and Westminster, like to commission publicly funded advertising campaigns. It gives the public the impression that the politicians they have elected to run the country are actually doing something. They also offer two distinct political advantages. Compared to passing legislation they can be produced very quickly and are highly visible. Second, ministers have complete control over them. Creating the appearance of a busy government working on your behalf is irresistible to media-savvy politicians and as BBC1's *Panorama* pointed out, it offers a reasonable explanation as to why the media spend on these campaigns regularly peaks in the months preceding parliamentary elections. Funny that.

After MSPs from the Conservative and Scottish National parties started to complain about the rising costs of Scottish Executive advertising, the then finance minister Andy Kerr promised to take control and reduce the budget. Having reached a peak of £13m in 2002/03 it fell back to just over £9m in 2003/04 but has since climbed again. All the politicians missed the point. It's not just the cost and effectiveness of the campaigns that are being questioned, but the existence of such campaigns in principle.

Are there alternatives to the growing use of advertising as a tool of government? Well, not if you believe that state interference is the solution to our social ills. Politicians who see the nanny state as justified in interfering in our private lives will continue to see these campaigns as a legitimate method of telling people how they should behave. The creatives in the ad agencies will naturally compete to produce the most imaginative and entertaining communications and some of the campaigns will be cute. But will they change our behaviour? Just as great marketing can't save a bad product, great advertising can't save a flawed initiative. Simply lecturing the public on how they should behave is doomed to fail. Some people point to the success of the drink driving campaign in changing public behaviour, and the public mood, but this campaign has been running for over 30 years. Now there are so many health campaigns that the focus is lost and our attention is distracted.

The natural lessons about healthy eating gathered from family life are far more valuable than anything the government can tell us. In many cases both parents in a family are working so a child's experience of making food in the kitchen may be limited or non-existent. The pressures on single parents can be even harder. Convenience foods are just that, a convenience, but they can disconnect children from the origins of the food they eat and when they become parents they have no experience of their own to pass on. The cycle needs to be broken and it has to start in the home or at school. But it has to be through education not coercion.

It is not even crucial to teach people how to boil an egg or peel a spud. What is more important is that they know that chips or mashed potatoes come from spuds and that eggs can make omelettes and soufflés, or be scrambled, fried, poached or soft boiled and chopped up in a mug with a dab of butter and a touch of salt and pepper, just like my mum used to give me for supper (with buttered toast soldiers for dipping). I have great faith in the ability of people to learn to cook for themselves. If I have a concern it's the disconnection that some people have between the food they are eating and where it came from. Without that understanding starting to cook will always come out of a packet or the microwave, encouraging the homogenised, pasteurised, processed food that we are told is bad for us. I'm not sure how bad it is for us but I certainly don't think such food tastes as good.

In schools what is needed is, rather like teaching children how to add and subtract, is to focus on the basics from showing people what vegetables actually look and feel like, then getting them to chop, grate and eat it, raw and cooked. When Jamie Oliver famously flashed a leek at some school kids and asked them what it was, the answers included carrot and potato. No-one said a leek! I'm certainly not advocating a food nanny to mould children's health or shape their bodies. I merely want to end their ignorance and give them some basic skills so they can make their own choices. It's not nannying to suggest that schools teach children how to read or write, paint or sing, so what's the problem with children learning more about food?

I mention vegetables not because I have anything against meat (I love my meat!) but because it's the easiest place to start and there are so many dishes that are enhanced by a vegetable accompaniment, such as fennel baked in cream with parmesan grated on top of honest to goodness mashed tatties (maybe with some garlic butter and caramelised onions through them). Meanwhile advertisements that tell people that fish is a healthy option fail to recognise that many people are unfamiliar with a fish that hasn't already been filleted. Some kids don't even know that chicken drumsticks are a chicken's legs!

The state cannot help intervening, often when its help is least required. You might think that flying the Union Jack from the town hall would be an easy enough task but you would be wrong. Calne Town Council in Wiltshire caused dismay and uproar in equal measure when it decided it would allow volunteers to hoist the flag but accompanied this by introducing a new 50-point health and safety document that would prevent anyone with specific physical ailments from going on to the roof. This included anyone above the age of 60, excluding at a stroke practically all the members of the local British Legion, and certainly anyone who had served in the Second World War. John Ireland, the Legion's local branch chairman and a local councillor, told the *Daily Telegraph*, "We have fought bravely and many of us have risked our lives in a world war so we are perfectly capable of going up a ladder a few feet to put a flag up on a roof. It is absolutely ridiculous to be talking about health and safety. All the council is trying to do is stop us flying the flag."[4]

Such bureaucratic behaviour is not limited to Britain. In Salisbury, New Brunswick, Canada, officials displayed a similarly unbending approach. The Macintyre family thought it would be a great idea to build a tree house. The two young boys, Hunter and Duncan Macintyre, were excited with the prospect of the games they could play in it and the sleepovers they might have. Unfortunately, after their father had built it, the officials of Greater Moncton Town Planning Commission said they would have to pull it down, citing the lack of a permit.

This sort of thing happens all the time in Britain. People build extensions to their homes and fall foul of planning regulations and often have to tear it down when retrospective permission is not forthcoming. I don't intend to go over the behaviour of planning committees and what they do and don't allow on people's private property. That could take up another book. What I found interesting about the episode in Canada was that even if the Macintyres had applied for a permit (they had in fact asked and had been told that it wasn't necessary) they would have been allowed to build their tree house, but only on the ground.

The rules of Greater Moncton Town Planning Commission stipulated that for safety reasons any tree house must be built at ground level, ensuring it is in fact not a tree house at all. The mother told the local paper, *The Times and Transcript*, of utter confusion at the authority when they asked what they should do. "The first person there told us we didn't need a permit for a tree house, then another guy came out of his office and told us we did need one. He told us it would fall under the same by-law that covers garages and carports. We were told that we could have the tree house, but it would have to come down and out of the tree. In other words, the structure must be on the ground."

Speaking of the benefits of the tree house she said: "The kids are young, having fun and they're not hurting anyone. It's a good place for them to hang out. I know where they are and I can see them all of the time. They're away from the street so I know they're safe."[5] The authorities refused to comment other than to say that the tree house violated local codes and would be dealt with in the proper and legal way.

Nanny is quick to deny children the pleasures of a tree house and reprimand those who choose to cartwheel in the school grounds.[6] There is far less concern for the feelings and self-esteem of so-called fat kids who don't adhere to the 'norm'. Rebuked in public for their obesity and punished by being removed from their parents and forced to attend diet classes (or 'fat camps'), the classroom stigma attached to being overweight will become far worse than it ever was. Children can be cruel and the intervention of the state is likely to make the lives of children who are overweight even more miserable.

The lengths to which the state will try to alter our behaviour appear to be inexhaustible. They include not just what we eat and drink but how we carry it home and dispose of it. Take the use of plastic bags. A favourite idea attractive to green politicians is to tax plastic bags in order to penalise our behaviour. Readers may be familiar with the fact that such a tax was introduced in the Republic of Ireland a number of years ago and it has resulted in a 90 per cent drop in the issuing of plastic bags by shops. On the face of it that's quite an impact, but what has really happened? Well, first, we should recognise that the levy of 10p on every plastic bag issued to a customer by a shop was not intended to raise revenue for the Irish authorities, and it hasn't. The tax was environmentally inspired, the idea being to discourage the use of plastic bags so that less of them ended up buried in landfill sites or, as urban mythology has it, blowing about in the wind. To that extent, then, it has been successful. What it does not do is raise revenues for local councils because, as customers started to provide their own bags, trolleys or boxes, the extra revenue barely covers the cost of collecting it. The idea of putting a tax on plastic bags to raise money might be superficially attractive but if politicians have any sense they will bin it.

It should also be understood that it hits poorer families hardest. Old ladies, widowers, students and the genuine unemployed end up paying the levy when they do their shopping but they don't have a car to get to the shops and back. Meanwhile the environmentally conscious, guilt-ridden middle classes turn up at the Co-op or Waitrose in their 4x4 gas-guzzlers and simply load their green plastic boxes that fit snugly in the back and drive home, content that they have done their bit for the planet.

Okay, but at least the idea has environmental benefits? Sadly, when you dig beneath the surface all is not what it seems. One only has to ask what people actually do with their plastic bags to find out that the most important rule of all, the law of unintended consequences, has resulted in more plastic being used in Ireland than before. The reason is simple. The majority of people reuse their carrier bags, most often to put the household rubbish in before putting it into bigger plastic bin-bags or into the wheelie bins and containers that we've come to know and 'love'. Now, without the small plastic bags at their disposal, Irish families have had to purchase far more bin bags for their rubbish, a whopping 200 per cent more. We know this because the people who make small plastic bags are the same who make or distribute larger bin bags, and they keep sales records of both.

The alternative, brown paper bags, are not only less reliable, they are heavier. The extra weight makes the cost of bulk transport considerably greater with the result that some stores have chosen to bin the plastic bag without offering a replacement. Others, such as Marks & Spencer and Waitrose, offer 'bags for life' that you can buy and they will replace. So yet again the market adjusts to consumer demand or, more likely than not, tries to anticipate consumer demand in the fear that they will lose custom if they don't look environmentally conscious enough.

Westport, Connecticut, became the first East Coast jurisdiction in the United States to ban plastic shopping bags with a $150 fine for any retailer who dared to offer a plastic bag to customers. Seattle, Washington, is due to introduce a 20 cent plastic bag tax this year. The problem is, the arguments favouring paper over plastic bags are not clear cut. An estimated 1,000 billion plastic bags are consumed worldwide each year. Plastics do not biodegrade, they photo degrade, a process that requires sunlight to break down plastic into ever smaller pieces. If, under a landfill site, they don't degrade they stay inert contributing nothing to the atmosphere. Paper bags generate 70 percent more air pollutants and 50 times more water pollutants than plastic bags. 2,000 plastic bags weigh 30 pounds; 2,000 paper bags weigh 280 pounds making the transport costs (and pollution) greater, and the latter takes up a lot more landfill space. It also takes 91 percent less energy to recycle a pound of plastic than it takes to recycle a pound of paper and it takes more than four times as much energy to manufacture a paper bag as it does to manufacture a plastic bag.[7] Despite this, and not for the first time, politicians have decided to intervene to change people's behaviour through taxation or prohibition.

These examples show that nanny had matured far beyond making sure we didn't kill or injure other people. She also wanted to make sure we didn't kill or injure ourselves. Worse, she wanted to make sure we couldn't do the most innocuous things such as somersaults and cartwheels in the playground, hoist our nation's flag on the town hall roof or use plastic bags to take home our free trade humus and organic yoghurt. But the politicians were still not satisfied because we continued to grumble, protest and rebel. Nanny, it seemed, wasn't working. It was time to get tough. It was time to let loose the bully in the political playground.

Notes:
1. Lawrence of Arabia, Sir Hugh Cairns, and the origins of Motorcycle helmets. Neurosurgery-online.com
2. mag-uk.org
3. *Sikhs in Britain: The making of a community*, Gurharpal Singh and Darshan Singh Tatla, Zed Books, 2006 ISBN 1842777173
4. *Daily Telegraph* 26 July 2008
5. *Times & Transcript*, 9 July 2008
6. Nannyknowsbest.blogspot.com
7. reusablebags.com and libertyalert.blogspot.com

# Chapter Three

# THE BULLY STRUTS FORTH

*The whole aim of practical politics is to keep the populace alarmed (and hence clamorous to be led to safety) by menacing it with an endless series of hobgoblins, all of them imaginary.'*

- HENRY LOUIS MENCKEN

The extent to which the state can exert its authority is generally unappreciated by the British public. An Englishman's home is his castle has for a long time been a completely empty and valueless cliché. On Tuesday 15 July 2008 the Home Office issued to members of parliament a list showing the powers of entry available to various authorities. In 2007 there were 266 powers of entry but within a year this had climbed to a staggering 430, despite the fact that during his short-lived honeymoon period as Britain's new prime minister, Gordon Brown had announced that he would have a bonfire of petty rules.[1]

As usual words were cheap and Brown's government was soon introducing a further 16 new laws that allow snoopers and prosecutors to gain entry and rummage around in our drawers, attics, aviaries, lock-ups, kennels and kitchen cupboards. Clipboard touting officials can demand to know if we are keeping rabbits, have a fridge with the correct EU rating, a TV, or whether we are practising hypnotism illegally. We have to reveal if our hedges are too high, our imported plants have the right documents, or any pests.

No doubt arguments can be made for all of these powers. One would like to think that they were properly debated in the Houses of Parliament, although due to the lack of parliamentary time and the fact that many of these powers emanate from Europe, I rather doubt it. One cannot expect the British public to appreciate much of this because people don't, by and large, spend time reading the Anti-Social Behaviour Act or the Energy Information Household Refrigerators and Freezers Regulations 2004.

The growth in these powers represents our acceptance, indeed our reliance, on the state for acting and interfering in our everyday lives. It doesn't seem to be enough to provide laws that allow neighbours to settle disputes between themselves (such as enormous hedges). No, we demand that the state acts as a superannuated-arbiter with powers that allow it to police and even bully us. Such authority resting in a reasonable person can be considered non-threatening, but how often do we find that the people occupying such roles are, at best, short-tempered from handling the burdens placed upon them or, at worst, revel in their ability to bully us into submission? And this bullying is no coincidence. The state has, I contend, given up on nannying in favour of outright coercion as it sets itself ever greater targets – in our best interests, of course.

It is true that in Britain we laugh at some of the litigious battles that take place between individuals, or individuals and corporations, in the United States, but at least they are about rights and obligations between parties that are settled without recourse to the state. In Britain we placidly accept that when the inspector calls he or she will gain entry.

Political hope is always on the horizon but it should never be taken for granted. When Eric Pickles, the then local government spokesman for the Conservatives, said: "We will cut unnecessary powers of the state to enter homes, starting with council tax inspectors' right of entry"[2], many people cheered. But will these fine words translate into action? The history of politicians making easy promises to roll back the powers of the state is long and colourful. Eric Pickles has a reputation for being a good campaigner who delivers. We can only hope that he retains this responsibility in any future Tory government and can be pressed to meet his promises. It is all too easy for a different politician to come into the job and change his priorities; or, more likely, the new man resembles a rabbit caught in the headlights of his officials as they bear down on him with a juggernaut of files defending all that's gone before, then doing nothing and being flattened to become yet another example of political road kill.

Eric Pickles should speak to Dora Panagi. A fashion boutique owner in Muswell Hill, north London, Mrs Panagi experienced a 'raid' on her shop while serving customers because she had used the wrong colour of bin bags. Fined £300 (£75 for each bag) by the local Haringey council, she said officials burst in, accused her of committing a "crime" and that she could end up going to court and even get a criminal record. She argued that the council would not provide her with enough of the grey ones for commercial waste and so had to provide her own black ones herself. The council eventually backed down and dropped the fine. However, the bitter aftertaste of these bully state tactics will take a long time to go away, she said.[3]

Gordon Brown's government wants to go even further. New powers that would allow councils to fine residents £100 for leaving their bin out too long, rising up to £5000 and a criminal record if not paid within two weeks, are to be given a trial in the north of England. Council workers will patrol the streets looking for bins that have not been put away after collection or are left out in the wrong place. Fines could also be issued if the bins are not put in allocated spaces, are too far from the curb, not outside a gate or are put out too early.

In California the local authorities in San Francisco are preparing to go even further. It has been proposed that garbage collectors should be allowed to inspect San Francisco residents' trash to make sure that pizza crusts aren't mixed in with chip bags or wine bottles. Potential fines of up to $1,000 can be levied with garbage collection withdrawn for repeat offences. Trash would have to be separated and put into the correct bin; blue for recycling, green for compost and black for trash. San Francisco currently has a 70 per cent recycling rate without these fines but it wants to achieve a 100 per cent rate by 2020. Other American cities such as Pittsburgh and San Diego have mandatory recycling. None of them however require the composting of all food waste. Applying the scheme in apartment buildings will be especially difficult. "How do you determine which tenant is at fault?" asked Sean Pritchard of the San Francisco Apartment Association. "Or do we indiscriminately start fining all tenants for one tenant's poor judgment?" San Francisco has a reputation for intervention, having outlawed smoking in parks and feeding pigeons in much of the city.

Politicians are not immune from the new bullying, and that includes those who voted for the smoking ban. The old phrase "the biter bitten" becomes the bully bullied, for politicians are nothing if they are not cannibals, killing and consuming their own. And so it was with the resignation of Welsh culture minister Rhodri Glyn Thomas who, having voted to introduce a smoking ban in Wales, one evening walked into a Cardiff pub forgetting that he had a lit cigar in his hand. When this was politely pointed out to him by staff at the Eli Jenkins bar he courteously withdrew and went outside.

It was too late. He had crossed the line. No comment was more spiteful or unforgiving than that of one opponent who said: "The smoking ban was introduced in the interests of public health to protect people from the risk of smoking-related illnesses. There can be no exceptions to the rules and Rhodri Glyn Thomas would have been fully aware of that fact."[4] Why couldn't they just have said, "It's an easy mistake to make and must happen to a dozen or so people every night of the week. As soon as Rhodri realised his mistake he left the premises so nothing more should be made of it."

But that's not what was said. Bullies like to put the boot in when a man's down. One could argue that an example had to be made of Thomas, and that politicians who make laws should obey laws. But should one also not expect a degree of proportion in the prosecuting of laws? Would we have expected a judge, a policeman or a traffic warden to resign if they had walked inadvertently into a pub with a lit cigarette in their hand? Indeed, would we have expected those smoke police, the environmental health authorities, to have pressed for the prosecution of a nurse, a social worker, or a fair-trade coffee grower if they had done the same as Thomas and left the pub in obvious embarrassment? No, of course not.

There was no suggestion that Thomas was going to be fined the £50 fixed penalty, after all. If a member of the public, or a minister of the Crown driving his own car, pulls up on a double yellow line would we not expect a traffic warden to say, "You can't stop here, sir. Could you move along now?", only issuing a ticket if he stupidly refused to do so? The point to be drawn from this story is simple. It mattered not that it was a mistake, that there was no motive and there were no victims. Any public challenge to the smoking ban, and this was very public by the nature of his position, would be dealt with harshly. Bullies pick on weak opponents to scare others off. Thomas was in a very weak position because of previous gaffes (a few weeks earlier he had very publicly named the wrong person as the winner of Wales Book of the Year Award) so he was easy prey. As an ordained minister of the cloth Thomas must wonder what happened to forgiveness and Christian charity.

Bullying does not have age limits either. The National Children's Bureau, a government advisory group that receives nearly £12 million a year of taxpayers' money from various sources, has called on toddlers as young as three to be singled out for criticism if they display racist attitudes.[5] Nursery teachers, nurses, playgroup leaders and child minders should record and report any 'racist incident' by children in their care. In the past the NCB has campaigned for the criminalisation of smacking and it runs the Sex Education Forum, which wants more sex education in schools.

The bureau's 366-page guide, *Young Children and Racial Justice*, tells nursery staff: "No racist incident should be ignored. When there is a clear racist intent, it is necessary to be specific in condemning the action." Whilst I would agree with the document's guidance that "If children reveal negative attitudes the lack of censure may indicate to the child that there is nothing unacceptable about such attitudes", I fail to see the benefit of recording and reporting such incidents to the authorities. The care should be left to the nursery staff and if there's a problem they should report it to the parent not the council. Nevertheless, nurseries, just like schools, are told to report as many racist incidents as possible to local councils. The report goes on: "Some people think that if a large number of racist incidents are reported, this will reflect badly on the institution… in fact, the opposite is the case." Oh yeah? Pull the other one.

I am reminded of an incident that happened to one of my sons at primary school when he was eight-years-old. Amid some cheeky but not unfriendly banter, a coloured girl in his class called one of his friends, who was a little spotty, a name – saying his face was like a Smarties donut. My son, thinking that this was unfair, decided to defend his pal and said her face was like a chocolate donut. The girl, not liking a taste of her own name calling, decided to tell teacher that she had been called a chocolate donut and my son was duly reported for a racist incident. It was recorded in a book, he was given a 'yellow card' and had to talk about it with the rest of the class in what's commonly known as 'circle time'. (The children get in a circle and discuss a moral question raised by the teacher about their behaviour towards each other.) The girl was treated as a victim if not a saint.

My son had never displayed any previous prejudice against this girl or any coloured child and I have absolutely no doubt that had she not insulted his pal he would never have developed her metaphor and slung it back at her. Still, it became a statistic and a test for my son and it's fair to say that relationships with the girl were impaired rather than improved.

I'm not trying to make light of the issue. When such Big Brother bullying of children moves from nursery into primary school it can have serious consequences. After calling a mixed race eleven-year-old friend 'Paki' and 'Bin Laden' in a school playground argument, a boy of ten was taken to court in Salford. Despite the two lads subsequently making up and becoming friends again, the Crown Prosecution Service pressed ahead with the case because the victim's mother had made a complaint. The accused appeared at Salford Youth Court in 2006 where he denied a racially motivated offence under the Public Order Act of using threatening, abusive or insulting words or behaviour with intent to cause another person harm or distress. The district judge, Jonathan Finestein, ordered the authorities to review their decision to prosecute and the case was dropped. The judge said: "I'm not condoning what he supposedly said but there must be other ways of dealing with this apart from criminal prosecution."[6]

As well as coercion and stigmatisation there is the other symptom of a bully state, a complete unwillingness to let opponents have a voice. In the eyes of the bully state and its representatives, opponents are working against their own and the public's interests and do not deserve to be heard. So, not content with passing legislation to ban smoking in public places or other practices they disapprove of, the bullies try to silence the opposition. Behaving like the totalitarian regimes we all thought had been defeated when Western capitalism triumphed over bankrupt state socialism, anyone who speaks out against the bullies is likely to be told to shut up or, if they persist, made to shut up.

What happened to Simon Clark, director of the smokers' rights group Forest, is a good example of the bully state in action. In March 2008 Clark was invited to attend a meeting in Brussels, organised by SANCO, the European Commission's health and consumer protection unit. The meeting was described as a "stakeholder consultation on the Commission's smoke-free initiative" and the meeting was billed as being for "EU experts, civil society and social partners to support the Commission's Impact Assessment on the forthcoming initiative on smoke-free environments". Let me repeat that. It was a meeting for 'stakeholders' to assess the impact of planned smoke-free environments across Europe. As a representative of Europe's oldest lobby group for smokers, Clark's participation should have been indispensable. Not a bit of it. Several anti-tobacco campaigners who were also invited to attend the meeting called for him to go or they would leave the meeting. Not a single person, including representatives from some of the world's leading pharmaceutical companies, defended his right to be at the meeting.

Clark described it in his blog: "I sensed, as soon as I entered the room and introduced myself ('Hello, I'm Simon Clark, from the smokers' lobby group Forest'), that there could be trouble. The guy from Pfizer (yes, the pharmaceutical company) didn't look pleased, and there were mutterings from some of the other delegates. (There were around 20 in all.) No surprise then, when, as soon as the meeting began, and we had all formally identified ourselves, two or three hands shot up. As I suspected, some of my fellow delegates were none too happy that a representative of Forest was in the room. If I didn't leave, said one, she would. Others nodded their heads in agreement.

"The chairwoman looked at me. 'Sorry,' I said, 'I'm not trying to be difficult because I know some of you have come a long way for this meeting, but Forest represents adults who choose to smoke and tolerant non-smokers like me. The consumer is entitled to be represented in the political process. So, on a point of principle, I'm not going to leave.'"[7]

That was how it stood until the chairwoman suggested a compromise. Clark could stay for the presentation but he would have to leave for the duration of the "facilitated discussion". (For some reason the anti-smoking campaigners didn't want Clark to hear what they had to say. So much for transparent, open government!) He could return to make his own contribution but only after the meeting had effectively finished. Clark agreed to this compromise, explaining: "I suppose I could have stood my ground and refused to go, but to what purpose? The meeting would have broken up and they would have reconvened at a later date in my absence."[8]

Meanwhile Conservative MEP Roger Helmer has revealed that anti-smoking lobbyists would like to go even further. Incredibly, the bullies want to ban members of the European Parliament from even talking to tobacco companies.[9] The idea that legislators should make laws that effect people's rights, employment and property without listening to all sides of the debate is a huge challenge to an open society. The idea that a legitimate industry could face punitive action without being able to talk to the legislature is an affront to the democratic process.

As Helmer commented on his blog: "If we start with tobacco, where do we stop? Many of my colleagues would like to start restricting the drinks industry. They believe that 'Big Oil' is frustrating their attempts to curb global warming, packaged food companies contribute to obesity, cars cause accidents and pollute the atmosphere... This could grow into a full-scale assault on business and capitalism - which of course is exactly what many in the green lobby want."

We can only hope that the idea is dismissed out of hand but the very fact that anti-tobacco lobbyists are arguing for their opponents to be denied a voice in the political process demonstrates just how far the bully state is prepared to go to win this particular war.

Censorship comes in many shapes and sizes. Homosexual rights activist Peter Tatchell celebrated in March 2008 when the blasphemy laws were abolished saying: "We have won an important victory for free speech … The blasphemy laws are now a dead letter." If it was a victory then it was a perverse one because Tatchell and others like him have their own blasphemies they wish the state to adopt and enforce.

I am reminded of The Who's seminal warning of revolutions being false dawns in 'Won't Get Fooled Again': "Meet the new boss, same as the old boss".[10] Censorship has not gone away, it is just the censors that have changed, and given that there has not been a single successful prosecution under the blasphemy laws since 1977 it is fair to say the new kids on the block are keener and meaner than those they have replaced.

It is in the arts that we constantly see free speech and freedom of expression sacrificed on the altar of self-censorship. And if writers, artists and directors won't do it themselves then the bullying will lead to it being done to them such as when BBC Radio 1 cut the word "faggot" from the Pogues' song 'Fairytale of New York' with Tatchell's enthusiastic support. "The word faggot is being sung as an insult, alongside scumbag and maggot," he said. "In this abusive context it is unacceptable ... It is shameful that BBC Radio 2 and other radio and TV stations continue to play the full version with the word faggot included. It shows that they don't take homophobic language as seriously as racist language"[11]

Because free speech is now under assault in the name of seemingly progressive causes such as defending oppressed minorities, whether lesbians and gays, ethnic minorities or women, opposition can be muted. Brighton and Hove Council used new licensing laws in December 2007 to ban any art form said to incite hatred. This resulted in a Jamaican dance hall and reggae artists being outlawed for their "gay hating" homophobic lyrics. Some minorities might consider this a victory but the same laws could easily be used against them one day. Far better, surely, to use the power of reason and superior argument to ridicule and defeat ignorance and bigotry?

Many will recall Birmingham Rep having to halt performances of Gurpreet Kaur Bhatti's "blasphemous" and "deeply offensive" play *Bezhti* in 2005 after Sikhs protested outside and violence was threatened. At the National Theatre, Britain's premier drama house and the one that sets the tone for the nation, director Nicholas Hytner said the only way he would consider putting on a play that attacked Islam was if it was written by a Muslim. What, like Salman Rushdie? No chance. An adaptation of Aristophanes' *Lysistra* set in Muslim heaven was cancelled by the Royal Court Theatre and every time Shakespeare's *Merchant of Venice* is performed you can be sure the theatre will be forced to justify its decision.

This is not about religion itself. It's about political activists using religion to intimidate us, just as others use public health and health and safety. I may not agree with what various people put in their songs, their plays, their street theatre, but I neither fear it nor would I ban it. To do so is to strike a serious blow against free speech and freedom of expression. People should be free to offend as well as to praise and without us defending that right, even though we may detest such views, weakens us all and leaves us open to becoming the next target.

Censorship has always been with us. Europe is not alone in embracing censorship. Censorship has been creeping into North America for years now and extends beyond so-called extremist political opinions and into unconventional academic views. In the USA the trend is for campus-wide bans of conservative politicians, military generals and shock jocks, but in Canada it has extended beyond the campus and into the church and the stage. Ironically it was some United States professors who launched a campaign in August 2008 protesting at plans by the American Political Science Association to re-evaluate its choice of Toronto for its 2009 conference, claiming that Canada's restrictions on free speech puts controversial academics at risk of being prosecuted.[12] The protest found support from scores of academics across the USA, including eminent scholars such as Harvard University's Harvey Mansfield and Princeton University legal philosopher Robert P George. The fear of prosecution came after Canada's human rights commission prosecuted a variety of seemingly ordinary people, including a clergyman speaking to his flock and a comedian telling some innocuous jokes that Bernard Manning would have thought insipidly weak.

In Britain the idea of Anti-Social Behaviour Orders (ASBOs) seemed attractive enough on the face of it but so bizarre has their use become that it doesn't take much of a leap to see how they could be used against anyone, especially as they can be issued outwith the courts. When an 87-year-old is given an ASBO just for being sarcastic to his neighbours one realises how ASBOs could be used to bully anyone who does not conform.

Faceless officials have been gaining powers to bully people for years. There are now hundreds if not thousands of them traipsing our streets looking for you to drop a cigarette butt or an apple core or dump your fridge. No witness is required; their word is sufficient to generate a fine. As with the problem of maintaining order on London's Underground, the response of using officials stems from an unwillingness to apply the properly manned policing that people have been crying out for years.

The bullying is intimidating enough in Britain but it extends across Europe too. The European Arrest Warrant, again a product of the response to 9/11, allows any country in the European Union to extradite someone in Britain for what is not a crime here. Given the way that most continental countries operate, that means that you can be arrested and imprisoned while the evidence against you is gathered. It doesn't have to be available for the extradition. This has already led to some cases of British subjects languishing in jails for alleged crimes that would not pass muster in Britain. The most absurd example though is that of Australian teacher Gerald Toben who was arrested in Britain on a warrant issued by Austria for a charge that is not a crime in Britain or Australia – holocaust denial.

All this pales in significance when the application of Britain's terrorism legislation is considered. Just wearing a t-shirt that criticises the government is enough to have you stopped under the Terrorism Act.[13] That's what happened to 80-year-old John Catt at the 2005 Labour Conference when his t-shirt called for Blair and Bush to be tried for war crimes. Isolated incident? No, 20-year-old Charlotte Denis was arrested for wearing a 'Bollocks to Blair' t-shirt (she refused to take it off because she only had a bra on underneath) while 60-year-old Tony Wright was given an £80 fixed penalty notice for trying to sell t-shirts with the same slogan. Apparently they caused "harassment, alarm and distress".[14]

I think back to the Eighties and the stuff people would wear featuring abusive slogans attacking Margaret Thatcher. How did we get by then? How does the USA survive with the absolute right to freedom of speech and no slander or libel laws? And yet for all we see people such as Catt, Denis and Wright being persecuted for peacefully arguing against a war, we can also observe the inability or unwillingness of the same authorities to deal with people such as Muslim cleric Abu Hamza or Muslim protestors outside the Danish embassy, all calling for the death of infidels.

The argument that the war on terror requires such extreme measures appears rather thin when we compare the current threat to that of the IRA through the Seventies and Eighties. Irish republicans in their various forms nearly managed to assassinate the prime minister Margaret Thatcher when they blew up her hotel in Brighton (resulting in nine deaths). They also mortar-bombed Downing Street, murdered Conservative MP Airey Neave inside his car in the House of Commons, shot or blew up other MPs such as Ian Gow, demolished buildings in the City of London, placed bombs that killed and maimed at Harrods, Regents Park, Manchester, Birmingham, Coventry and many other places – not to mention the devastation they caused in Ulster itself in places such as Omagh and Enniskillen. A total of 3,725 people lost their lives and a further 47,541 were injured. The threat was real and tangible but it didn't require identity cards or detention for 28 days without charge.

In addition to that seismic change we now see on-the-spot fines that can criminalise people if they refuse to pay, the suspension of habeas corpus, the right to a jury denied, the confiscation of property without a conviction, not to mention the surfeit of CCTV cameras that are appearing all over the country including, it is said, in people's private homes. You might think that, hang on, there is a real threat and we need some of these anti-terrorism laws to protect us. What a pity then that they were not passed with the sorts of checks and balances that would prevent local authorities using them to bully the people about how they put their bins out, or Gordon Brown using them to bring down an Icelandic bank – in our best interests, of course. The point is that if we allow politicians to have these types of powers they need to have clear and identifiable limits that need to be regularly approved, just as the anti-terrorism laws dealing with the IRA required renewal annually.

And so it goes on. The nannying of our lives has not just extended to cover our health, our work and our play, but it has become more heavily policed with ever stiffer penalties, leading to ordinary law-abiding citizens being turned into criminals simply because they have the audacity to say "No, my life is my own". In the next few chapters I shall look in more detail at smoking, eating, drinking and the surveillance state – what I call the front line. If we do not defend ourselves there, the capacity to bully us in public will be taken directly into the privacy of our homes.

Notes:
1. *The Sun*, 21 July 2008 'Home Invasion by the State'
2. *The Daily Telegraph*, 26 July 2008
3. *The Daily Telegraph*, 28 September 2008
4. BBC Wales News on line 18 July 2008 and Walesonline.co.uk 19 July 2008
5. *Daily Mail*, 7 July 2008
6. *Daily Mail*, 18 July 2008 and BBC News 18 July 2008
7. Simon Clark, The Free Society 2008
8. The participants at the meeting included the following: Pfizer, Novartis, Johnson & Johnson, GlaxoSmithKline (all pharmaceutical companies), Eurofound (European Foundation for the Improvement of Living and Working Conditions), InwatEurope (International Network of

Women against Tobacco), International Health and Social Affairs Office, NHS Health Scotland, Business Europe, EUN, HOTREC (representing hotels, restaurants and cafes in Europe), AESGP (Association of the European Self-Medication Industry), SFP (Smoke-Free Partnership) and EHN (European Heart Network).

9.   Post-darwinist.blogspot.com, 24 August 2008

10. 'Won't Get Fooled Again', Pete Townsend, 1971

11   BBC Online, Tuesday 18 December 2007

12. Taboo or not taboo, that is the question Claire Fox, The Free Society 28 March 2008

13. Anti-Terrorism, Crime and Security Act 2001

14. *The Rotten State of Britain*, Dr Eamonn Butler, Gibson Square, London 2009

# Chapter Four

# SMOKING STUBBED OUT

*"...the line between nannying and oppression*
*has become no wider than a cigarette paper.*
*Not that you will be allowed to buy one of those"*

## - DR EAMONN BUTLER

Establishing laws is a serious business and should not be taken lightly. Not only does it impact on millions of people's lives, it can turn people into criminals for behaving in a way that was previously considered acceptable. Worse, it can be counter-productive. The public smoking ban is one of many examples.[1] When the then Scottish first minister Jack McConnell told the Holyrood Parliament in 2004 that the ban was intended to protect children he must have known that it was entirely probable that instead of going to pubs smokers would simply stay at home and smoke – in front of the children!

It's not as if there were no warnings for McConnell and his colleagues. A 2004 survey of 2,071 people, carried out by YouGov for Churchill Home Insurance, revealed that more than half of Scottish smokers would shun pubs and bars if smoking was banned.[2] (It has probably not been as high as this but the trend is nevertheless well established.) Churchill warned that this could increase the risk of fires being caused by stray cigarettes. The company said it carried out the research because smoking in the home accounted for half of all its household fire claims. Martin Scott, the company's head of home insurance, said: "This research clearly shows that people's habits will change if a ban was imposed. With over half of Scottish smokers pledging to stay away from bars and smoking more at home, we could well see more incidents of cigarette-related house fires."

On 15 September 2009 the Scottish *Daily Mail* reported that: "The number of people killed in house fires caused by smokers has risen dramatically since smoking was banned in public places." Accidental house fires started by smoking materials doubled in 2007 following the introduction of the ban in Scotland in 2006. The paper quoted Simon Clark, director of the smokers' lobby group Forest: "I am saddened but not surprised at these figures – they show the law of unintended consequences that always accompany such prohibitions. We have always argued that the safest place to smoke tobacco is a well-ventilated bar or restaurant and that instituting a complete ban would inevitably cause problems. We would hope that MSPs would review the ban in light of these deaths. However, it is more likely that the health fanatics will use this as an excuse to crack down on smoking in the home. That would be almost impossible to enforce and amount to a gross infringement of civil liberties."

In the 2004 survey for Churchill Insurance, 54 per cent of Scots (40 per cent of the rest of the UK) said they would shun pubs and entertain more at home, while 29 per cent said they would drink more in public places to compensate for a lack of cigarettes; 19 per cent said they would smoke more, both before and after a night out on the town, and 17 per cent said the lack of cigarettes would make them eat more in restaurants and bars. These are not what one might call healthy outcomes but it's a typical example of the sort of unintended consequences that regularly come back to bite politicians. And so it came to pass. Smokers were outlawed from pubs and clubs and sought refuge in their homes. The smoking ban may not be the only factor in the decline of the British pub, but it can't be a coincidence that closures have increased dramatically in recent years and pubs in Britain are now closing at the rate of 52 a week.[3]

Attempts to introduce a smoking ban in Scotland began in earnest in 2004, shortly after the introduction of the ban in Ireland, when the recently re-elected Scottish Executive launched a consultation exercise on tobacco controls in a pub that was trying bravely to offer the choice of a smoke free environment. I say bravely because pubs that had gone smoke free prior to the ban had often struggled for public support, and this pub was no different. At the same the Scottish Parliament's Health Committee was taking evidence from various protagonists as it considered the merits of a private bill that would ban smoking in establishments that served food. The chance for politicians to grandstand by fulminating and wearing their fatuous indignation on their sleeves was too good an opportunity to miss. Smokers are a minority these days and in Britain at least they have shown a willingness to shrug their shoulders and find other places to smoke. Politicians took the view that they might not be a pushover but they could be pushed.

Ironically a king size exocet was delivered by the then English health secretary John Reid (a Scot with a Scottish seat). Reid angered health campaigners on both sides of the border when he declared: "I just do not think the worst problem on our sink estates by any means is smoking, but it is an obsession of the learned middle class. What enjoyment does a 21-year-old single mother of three living in a council sink estate get? The only enjoyment sometimes they have is to have a cigarette." [4]

Reid's comments ignited a storm of protest. Deborah Arnott, director of Action on Smoking and Health (ASH), said: "If John Reid's contribution to the White Paper on smoking is let the poor smoke, then his policy on obesity must be let them eat cake." Andrew Lansley, the Tory health spokesman, accused Reid of undermining the government's health promotion message. Paul Burstow, the Liberal Democrat health spokesman, said: "This is yet more evidence that the health secretary has no clue when it comes to public health. His statement is patronising, damaging and based on weak assumptions." Burstow added that Reid, a former 60-a-day man (so he had some experience of smoking), should "stop making these shallow comments and come out in favour of a smoking ban in public places". Only Forest praised the health secretary for starting a "more balanced debate".[5] Nevertheless Reid had struck a chord and he remains one of the few politicians in Britain who has had the courage to speak up and say what is manifestly true.

Meanwhile New York was hailed in Scotland and elsewhere as a role model for countries that wanted to ban smoking in public places. Introduced in 2003 the New York ban was said to provide evidence from tax revenues that businesses in the hospitality trade were witnessing a sales growth rather than the feared decline. This argument told us nothing because the growth could be accounted for by the recovery from the tourism slump that followed the 9/11 tragedy in 2001. In fact many bar owners were reporting staff redundancies and it is more likely that while the wider New York hospitality trade such as hotels, tourist attractions and restaurants were experiencing a growth, the bars that introduced the smoking ban were experiencing a downturn.

In Ireland, where a public smoking ban had been introduced in March 2004, some Dublin publicans displayed typical bravado by turning the new laws to their advantage, installing outdoor heaters and encouraging a continental atmosphere for their smoking clientele to relax and share the craic outdoors. But this was Ireland, land of the lock-in. With only 40 inspectors to police the new laws, who could doubt that when the Guinness was still flowing at two in the morning in a rural idyll the fag would still be hanging on the edge of the bartender's mouth and the off-duty Gardai police officer he was serving might be lighting up his fourth filter tip?

That's why the Irish were so relaxed about the whole process, at least in advance of the ban. Introduce the same law in Scotland, I thought, and with Calvinist relish a whole regiment of blue meanies would be hired to march into every bar and bothy from Wick to Wigtown. The reality though was that policing was left to landlords who found themselves forced to become a proxy police force through the threat of large fines and the fear of losing their licences if anyone lit up on their premises. Coupled with our traditional law-abiding attitude, it was no surprise when Scotland's ban was received with grumbling shrug of resignation.

Those against the ban argued that it was a matter of choice and that while they were willing to concede bans in public spaces such as shopping malls and offices they believed that pubs, cafes and restaurants were in fact private spaces and it was for the proprietor to decide who could cross the threshold and whether or not they could smoke. Those favouring a ban argued that non-smokers, in particular the staff, have rights too and that the health risks from secondhand smoke are so great that even proprietorial rights can be superceded if the state decides that it is in "our best interests".

It seemed clear that supporters of a ban could only succeed if secondhand smoke could be shown to be the cause of serious ill health and even death. In the Scotland the Scottish Executive chose to present opinion as a fact. In the absence of any clear evidence we were told that 'passive smoking' was responsible for one thousand deaths in Scotland every year. In the UK as a whole it was said that 11,000 non-smokers died each year from secondhand smoke. Again, there was never any real evidence to support this claim but the bully state isn't interested in the truth. As far as government is concerned, the end justifies the means.

Concern for the health of bar workers and non-smokers in general was a red herring. Smoking bans are principally about the denormalisation of smoking. The aim is to isolate and shame smokers into submission by depicting them as anti-social or, worse, responsible for the deaths of the non-smokers with whom they share their lives. If smoking bans are simply to 'protect' the workers they could easily permit well-ventilated designated smoking rooms and give staff the option of not going in.

The persecution of smokers wasn't restricted to Scotland because Wales quickly followed suit. Following the introduction of a public smoking ban in Wales in April 2007 a painter and decorator was astonished to receive a £30 on-the-spot fine for smoking in his own van because it was deemed to be his workplace. Gordon Williams, 58, from Llanafan, mid Wales, smoked ten cigarettes a day and was on the A487 near Aberystwyth when his Suzuki van was pulled over by Ceredigion council officials carrying out safety checks. He was out on an errand for his wife and had lit a cigarette before getting into his van and carried on smoking. Williams explained: "I was on my way to a shop to buy some teabags when the council official pulled me over. I was told that because my van is my place of work I had broken the smoking laws. I am dumbfounded. The van is only insured for private use and to get me to and from work. It is not my place of work. I decorate houses, not vans. I don't use it for work so I can't see how they can do me for smoking in the workplace." [6]

A supporter of the ban, Williams went on: "I respect anyone who chooses not to smoke but I would also ask for the same respect, to have the freedom to smoke in my own private vehicle." His wife Sue paid the £30 fine almost immediately believing that if it wasn't paid within a certain time limit it would double. She commented afterwards: "If you ask me they have overstepped the mark. I use the van myself for shopping trips. Does that mean I also couldn't smoke in there? It was a very expensive packet of teabags. It just doesn't make sense to us." Ceredigion Council defended the fine stating that the smoking legislation allows very few exemptions to the smoking ban and includes workplaces and work vehicles. A spokesman at the Welsh Assembly later challenged this interpretation saying: "Smoking is permitted in vehicles used for work purposes that are for the sole use of the driver and are not used as a workplace by anyone else."

It was with some irony that Labour subsequently lost the Scottish Parliament elections by one seat because there is circumstantial evidence to believe that had it not introduced such a comprehensive ban it would still be in power in Scotland today. I'm not suggesting that a wave of anti-Labour hysteria gripped the nation because of the ban, but when a party loses power by one seat one has to look at the constituencies that it lost and there are two where the smoking ban could be said to have made an difference: Central Fife, where the voluble anti-smoking campaigner and Labour MSP Christine May lost her seat, and Cunninghame North, where Labour minister Alan Wilson lost his seat by just 48 votes. May's seat in Fife was the focus for opposition because some miners' welfare clubs saw their income go through the floor, while Cunninghame was home to the largest Labour social club in Scotland where members objected strongly to the ban. Although the SNP voted overwhelmingly for the ban it was careful to leave some mavericks free to exploit Labour's excessive legislation.

Maybe it was just coincidence but for Labour it was an avoidable one. If only McConnell had noticed that Fianna Fail also suffered significant political defeats immediately after introducing the Irish smoking ban. Whatever the reason, it certainly doesn't appear to be the vote winner that it is claimed to be. There is significant anecdotal evidence that this disconnection between Labour policy makers and politicians from their rank and file supporters is seriously damaging the party. The smokers' rights group Forest, for example, reports that one of the most common messages they get from smokers is: "I've always voted Labour, but never again".

In Westminster, unlike Holyrood, Conservative opposition to the ban was muted and the party granted its MPs a free vote. Labour had promised in its 2005 election manifesto to limit the ban with exemptions for private members' clubs and pubs that don't serve food. All of this was forgotten when in February 2006 Labour MPs voted overwhelmingly in favour of a comprehensive ban in England from July 2007, with a surprising number of Tory MPs joining them.

Since the introduction of the ban pub closures have increased dramatically. The ban also hit bingo halls. I've never been to a bingo hall (although I've played bingo many times in hotels on package holidays) but I know that an afternoon or an evening at the bingo is a great escape for many people. As far as I can tell, bingo's greatest attraction is the conviviality and the friendship, the gossiping and the banter. The evidence for this comes not just from people I know who are regulars but also from the business model that operates in bingo halls. Income is derived not just from the game itself but from soft drinks and food.

What has happened in bingo halls following the smoking ban is that players have been forced outside to have a smoke between games, with the result that they have stopped spending money inside the hall. As a result takings have plummeted and many independent bingo halls have closed. Even the big players, Gala Coral and Rank, have suffered. In 2007 Rank closed 17 bingo halls and Gala Coral has closed 16 bingo halls and four casinos since the ban was introduced. Industry analysts say this trend is set to continue and a combination of the smoking and recent tax changes could lead to a further 40-50 closures.[7]

Whatever the number, each closure leads to more people staying at home instead of going out socialising. For many people life becomes a duller, joyless, sadder affair. Politicians were warned by bingo operators that this would happen but, and I witnessed this with my own eyes, they were laughed at. Bingo was dismissed as the pursuit of working class plebs. Bullies never listen and they certainly don't play bingo.

It's not just publicans and bingo operators who are suffering. Hoteliers and restaurateurs have been affected, even taxi drivers. In Peebles, in the sleepy Scottish Borders, two part-time mini-cab drivers who used their own cars to drive passengers around had pulled over to have a break. The rain was pouring down so one got into the other's car and they had a puff and a natter. Nobody was about, not a soul. It was the wee sma' hours and nothing stirred. Eventually a call came in and one went off to pick up a customer. A couple of days later both men were visited by the police. Their names had been passed on by their cab office after the police had enquired about the drivers of the cars with the registration plates they had been watching with the help of the town's CCTV. Even though they had been sitting in their own cars, in their own downtime, they had been breaking the law. If you use your car for 'private hire' you cannot smoke in it at any time, even if you work in John O'Groats and are holidaying in Stranraer. It's a working environment and you can no longer light a cigarette inside.

It was the first week of the Scottish ban so the drivers were let off with a warning. Now during breaks they get out of their car and smoke rebelliously in a doorway, but every so often in Britain a cab driver is fined for smoking in his own car in his own time. In fact, if you're a cab driver in Britain you can't even smoke a cigarette if the door of the cab is open and you are standing within a foot or so of the vehicle in case a whiff of smoke should drift inside. A cabbie in Bedfordshire was fined for exactly that 'offence'. Now that's what I call a bully state.

The relentless alienation and persecution of smokers is set to continue. Anti-smoking campaigners have a long list of tobacco controls they want to introduce, sooner rather than later. They include a ban on smoking in cars where young children are present; a ban on smoking while driving (irrespective of the presence of children); a ban on the display of tobacco in all retail outlets with the exception of specialist tobacconists; a ban on smoking in beer gardens and open air parks plus exclusion zones around public buildings; a ban on tobacco vending machines; the introduction of a licensed retailer scheme; the introduction of plain packaging; the prohibition of ten-packs; and changing the classification of films in which people are smoking to an '18' certificate.

The list goes on. Some of them are just silly, like the proposed ban on ten-packs. The idea that this will reduce youth smoking is laughable. Young people will simply buy a pack of 20 and split them with a mate. Worse, in the absence of a ten-pack they will buy a packet of 20 and end up smoking more! As Dr Eamonn Butler, director of the Adam Smith Institute, argued in *The Times*, if small bars of chocolate were banned we'd buy a big one instead and eat the lot![8]

Perhaps the most damaging proposal, to small businesses if not smokers themselves, is the plan to ban the display of tobacco in shops. Many small stores rely on regular customers. Smokers don't just buy tobacco on a regular basis, they also buy their newspapers and milk and other sundry items. Restrict the sale of tobacco and small shops face severe financial difficulties. Unlike supermarkets they have no room for manoeuvre, no wriggle room to make up sales elsewhere. By forcing tobacco out of sight and under the counter, many smokers will go to the nearest supermarket which will stock more brands and offer a dedicated service.

This is not guesswork. When a similar ban was introduced in Saskatchewan in Canada, over 800 local shops are said to have closed down the following year. Combine that with the removal of cigarette vending machines and many local pubs and shops that are the currently hub of the community could be pushed into bankruptcy. And for what? Forced underground (or under the counter), smoking may become even more alluring for many teenagers. Consumption won't fall, at least not dramatically. It will simply be displaced into the black market where there are fewer controls and the temptation is to smoke other substances such as cannabis and crack cocaine.

Such controls take Britain ever closer to the point where tobacco is prohibited altogether, and that is clearly the long-term goal, but for now campaigners are happy to settle for what they call "the next logical step". Whether or not such oppressive intervention in the lives of consenting adults is justified depends on how much you believe your life is your own or that social engineering is acceptable.

The threat to the majority of us who don't smoke is that once these methods of denormalisation have been tried and tested on smokers it will be very easy for campaigners to move on and target other habits. If you like drinking alcohol it's already happening. Very soon campaigners may demand to put stronger beers or spirits below the counter. The carcinogens in kippers, real or imaginary, the cholesterol in chicken jaalfrezie or whatever else you fancy – fatty, smoked and salty foods – they'll be on the list too. Already one MP has tried to ban cartoon characters from cereal packets. Prohibiting personalities like Gary Lineker from promoting crisps will be next, all for our own good, of course.

What can't be refuted is that there is little empirical evidence to show that these intrusions in our lives actually work. The biggest fall in smoking rates in the UK happened when there were very few restrictions on people smoking in public places and we were still surrounded by tobacco advertising and sponsorship. People were informed about the health risks associated with smoking and many took the decision to quit. They didn't give up because they were made to feel guilty about their habit or turned into a social pariah. They made that decision for themselves.

Here are the facts: in the 1950s 80 per cent of men and 40 per cent of women smoked. By 1974 the percentage of the population who smoked had fallen to 45 per cent. Between 1974 and 1992 it fell to 28 per cent. Over the next decade or so, during which smoking was increasingly restricted in public areas, tobacco advertising and sponsorship was banned and tobacco taxation rose to record levels, the smoking rates fell by just three per cent. Since the introduction of the smoking ban, it is said to have fallen by a further two or three per cent but nothing dramatic.

Clearly a lot of smokers are digging in their heels and refusing to quit. Claire Fox, director of the Institute of Ideas, has argued that as a result of all the anti-smoking propaganda, she and many other smokers are "reaching for their fags in defiance". She's right. Indeed it's remarkable how often tobacco controls prove to be counter-productive. Take the banning of tobacco displays in Iceland, one of the few countries to have introduced such a law. Since the ban was introduced the incidence of youngsters smoking has generally remained unchanged and among teenage girls is now worse (rising from 64.8 per cent in 1995 to 69 per cent in 2001, to 71.6 per cent in 2006). This compares with other countries where there have been no such controls and yet youth smoking rates have fallen.

In the UK successive governments, Conservative and Labour, increased taxation on tobacco to such a degree that it led to a smuggling epidemic, the loss of over £3 billion in revenue, and the widespread availability of cheap and sometimes counterfeit cigarettes on the black market. (Needless to say, instead of reducing tobacco taxation to a more sensible level, the bully state chose to tackle the problem by increasing the number of officials and spending more money on scanning equipment in Britain's ports. Caught up in the crackdown on smuggling were thousands of innocent Channel shoppers who were merely indulging in their right to buy, import and consume cheaper tobacco from the continent for their own personal use.

Meanwhile the smoking ban has led to more people standing outside pubs and clubs, and that in turn has led to increased noise (so-called 'noise pollution') and more litter. Again, the bully state intends to 'solve' this problem not by giving smokers a designated smoking room inside but by introducing exclusion zones around public buildings. The most barbaric example of this can be seen around NHS hospitals where smokers, some of them patients, one or two attached to drips, are not allowed to smoke near the entrance and are increasingly banned from smoking anywhere on the hospital grounds. Nothing beats that as an example of the inhumanity of the bully state.

Anti-smokers don't talk much about Greece or Japan, heavy-smoking nations where people tend to live longer, healthier lives than in the UK. In Japan the smoking rates are higher but lung cancer is considerably lower, suggesting that there's far more to contracting cancer than we currently understand. Facts like these are simply ignored by anti-tobacco campaigners. Still, why should non-smokers care? The zealots have a dogma and mere facts and unhelpful human behaviour is an inconvenience to be ignored. The justification for the relentless persecution of smokers is distorted statistics and junk science.

Take the claims about smoking-related deaths or illnesses. In 1997 the Labour peer Lord Stoddart of Swindon, a champion of smokers' rights although not himself a smoker, asked the new Labour government what were the "so-called smoking-related diseases from which the government estimated 120,000 people [that is, smokers] die each year" and how many die at what ages? The answer was revealing because it clearly showed, in the eight types of cancer and eight other diseases including pneumonia and ischemic heart disease, that all the deaths from these 16 diseases could not solely be confined to smokers. Of the roughly 630,000 people who die every year in the UK, about 400,000 are from 'smoking-related diseases', but given the proportion of people who have smoked is about a third of the population, well over half of all deaths of non-smokers are from smoking-related diseases. As Ralph Harris puts it in his excellent book *Murder a Cigarette*: "The listed diseases turn out to be no more 'smoking-related' than a broken limb from a traffic accident can scrupulously be called a sporting injury."

More telling in the answer and more embarrassing to the anti-smoking bullies was that of the 400,000 estimated annual deaths from those 16 so-called smoking-related diseases, about 350,000 occur in the over 65s and about 220,000 occur in those who live beyond the average life expectancy of men (74) and women (79). So much for the claims about smokers' life expectancy being on average 20 years shorter than the average non-smoker.

So despite the unavailability of any evidence that can be scientifically accepted or proven in court we have fag packets that declare 'Smoking Kills' and advertising campaigns that, when they are not telling smokers that they stink, imply that they are killing their children and anyone else who comes into their vicinity. The abuse of statistics and the abuse of smokers tell us everything we need to know about the people who run the bully state. It's the only language they know.

Together with the distorted statistics comes a suppression of any study that suggests that nicotine might have some beneficial effects. My own life experiences tell me that practically all substances, be they pure elements (oxygen, say) or combinations of elements (water) can have a good or a bad effect depending on the dose. You can die from drinking too much water and you can die from not having enough. You can die from water in your lungs but not in your stomach. It is not the water that is deadly. It's what you do with it and how much you consume.

This is not rocket science. Everybody understands this fact. Take half an aspirin a day and it is said (although this is now disputed) that you will improve your chances of avoiding a heart attack because aspirin thins the blood. Take a couple every four hours and it should relieve the pain of a headache. Take 30 at once and you could end up in hospital having your stomach pumped. The poison, as I never tire of telling people, is the dose not the substance.

So it should be no surprise that if smoking has harmful effects then it might also have some mildly beneficial effects. Smokers tell me that it relieves tension, reduces stress and relaxes their mood. Given the stressful nature of modern life it is no surprise that many people like to reach for a packet of cigarettes, just as people drink coffee or open a bottle of wine. Some replace snacking (comfort food) with smoking. Rather than reaching for that Snickers bar some people light another cigarette. I've known people to go back on the fags for a couple of weeks just to lose weight, although like all diets not everyone finds it works for them. More seriously, there have been studies that have suggested that smokers may have a 50-70 per cent reduced risk of Alzheimer's disease, a 50 per cent reduced risk of Parkinsons disease and better prospects in contracting ulcerative colitis, rheumatoid arthritis and, yes, some cancers too (cancer of the uterus, for instance). When these studies are published, however, they are immediately jumped upon, rubbished and ridiculed.

This is typical bullying behaviour. No-one is allowed an alternative opinion. If anyone dares to challenge the modern orthodoxy they are shouted down. The best example of this took place in 2003 when the *British Medical Journal* published a study concerning secondhand smoke. This wasn't any old study. It was the largest of its kind and it had been peer reviewed and published by one of the world's leading medical journals. The study, by James Enstrom of the University of California, and Geoffrey Kabat of New Rochelle, New York, found that the link between environmental tobacco smoke and coronary heart disease and lung cancer may be considerably weaker than generally believed. They found that exposure to environmental tobacco smoke, as estimated by smoking in spouses, was not significantly associated with death from coronary heart disease or lung cancer at any time or at any level of exposure.

The authors received fearful abuse from the professional health lobby. Responding to the criticism, Enstrom and Kabat wrote: "Owing to the charged atmosphere surrounding the issue of passive smoking, our paper provoked strong reactions on bmj.com. The most disturbing reactions have come from the enforcers of political correctness who pose as disinterested scientists but are willing to use base means to trash a study whose results they dislike. They have no qualms about engaging in personal attacks and unfounded insinuations of dishonesty rather than judging research on its merits. The resulting confusion has misled many readers and diverted attention from the facts of the study." [9]

This is how the bully state works. Anyone who doesn't support 'the project' is isolated, abused and denormalised. No wonder so few people, whether they be doctors, scientists, journalists or politicians are prepared to stand up and fight back.

Who are they who harangue independent scientists or independent-minded politicians like John Reid? Well, thanks (inadvertently) to the National Audit Office we now know that the government conspired with health charities to create an atmosphere conducive to passing more tobacco controls. Reviewing a Department of Health report (Tobacco Control: The Power of

Partnerships), the NAO said: "This paper shows how the government, via a coalition of related intermediary brands (NHS, Cancer Research UK and British Heart Foundation), successfully changed smoking behaviour with each organisation offering a different reason to give up, in ways that did not victimise smokers.

"This case study demonstrates how engaging and working with intermediaries can complement a government department's communication effort, adding weight and variety to a campaign. It also demonstrates how using the provenance of outside organisations can add credibility to key messages. In 1998, the Department of Health unleashed a new assault on tobacco in the White Paper 'Smoking Kills'. The key objective of the paper was to help existing smokers to quit. A target was set to reduce adult smoking from 28 per cent to 21 per cent by 2010, with a fall to 26 per cent by 2005.

"To learn from international experience, DH reviewed some very successful smoking cessation campaigns from around the world. From Australia particularly the power of certain types of shock tactics was notable. DH then commissioned research which showed that the shock and anti-industry approaches performed very well with consumers, but there were two problems. First, the graphic visual style of the Australian campaign was felt to be too hard-hitting for the NHS brand and second, government messages exposing the industry were counterproductive and viewed as hypocritical in England. There was a strong desire to avoid smokers feeling 'victimised' by too many 'government warnings'.

"The breakthrough to resolve these problems was to engage powerful intermediaries who would be willing to become a credible voice for these two approaches. In November 2002, DH took the radical step of committing £15m over three years to fund tobacco control campaigns from charities, including Cancer Research UK (CRUK) and The British Heart Foundation (BHF).

"CRUK agreed to reveal the truth (sic) behind the tobacco industry's 'light' and 'mild' tobacco descriptors. Their 'Death

Repackaged' campaign successfully used dangerous animals with cosy names to illustrate the idea that just because 'low tar' cigarettes have nice names such as 'lights' or 'mild' doesn't mean they are any less dangerous. There is proof that the CRUK branding specifically increased the impact of communication: 67 per cent of smokers agreed that the advertising 'really caught' their attention; but if smokers were aware it was from Cancer Research UK, 84 per cent found it attention grabbing. This clearly demonstrates the strength of using charities as an independent credible voice.

"BHF brought its authority to the link between smoking and the heart in a new and graphic way with their award-winning 'give up before you clog up' campaign. Like the CRUK element of the overall campaign, the BHF activity was also proven to have a dramatic effect in changing smoking behaviour among consumers."

In other words the Department of Health used charities to say things the government did not want to say publicly (for fear of being accused of victimising smokers). The charities also brought a degree of credibility to the debate that the government did not have. The money given to these charities is in addition to the hundreds of thousands of pounds that governments in Westminster and Holyrood give to Action on Smoking and Health and ASH Scotland respectively every year. (ASH Scotland now employs a staggering 27 people, mostly paid for by the taxpayer.)

Sometimes the bully state employs outright duplicity. In September 2009 the *Guardian*, which can hardly be called a friend of the smoker having supported most of the anti-tobacco measures of the last decade, revealed how government ministers continued to claim that the cost of installing the new 'under cover' tobacco displays would be "as little as £120" per shop, ignoring communications from a Canadian manufacturer of cigarette display cases which made clear that the cost would be considerably more because it didn't include factors such as delivery and installation. The real costs are expected to be between £1,850 and £4,985 per shop but the Department of Health didn't want the people to know that.[10]

Joe Jackson, the musician and writer, wrote in 2008 that the UK was one of the worst places in the world to be a smoker. "It's awful, worse even than that Kremlin of the anti-smoking empire, the USA. But that was before I found myself in the place where bad smokers go when they die. I have been to Hell, and its name was Brisbane."

When Jackson toured Australia a quarter of a century ago he liked the city. Now, he reports, it has been infected by a combination of American-style health freakery and an intolerant, British-style nanny state. In Brisbane, he wrote, it's illegal to smoke anywhere food or drink is served or consumed, including at outside tables. Sometimes there's an area 15 feet away where smokers can spark up, but where it is illegal to take one's drink. Jackson noticed something that I have witnessed in other countries like the USA. Cities compete with one another to introduce the most severe restrictions. "I was in Sydney, it had fairly tough restrictions, but Brisbane was relatively liberal," he wrote. "Now, having 'lagged behind' before, it wants to show how 'tough' it can be." [11]

Jackson's European tour in 2008 led him to pen a couple of articles detailing what smoking laws he found in the many countries he played in. It provided a useful and entertaining way of revealing how practically every country is different and how Britain is possibly the most intolerant nation in Europe.

In France, Paris witnessed a demonstration of 10,000 people against the country's public smoking ban. (The British media studiously ignored it.) Fortunately the French were able to fall back on one of the fine inventions that this cultured country gave to the world, the terasse, which Jackson reported are largely enclosed and enjoy decorative heaters that are becoming attractive accoutrements in their own right. The effect has been to pack the streets and empty the bars.

In Belgium smoking is banned in restaurants but not bars. I always liked Brussels and Bruges and look forward to reacquainting myself with them to enjoy my pipe and cigars in peace. In Holland, Amsterdam is struggling, struggling with its own self-imposed contradiction that you can no longer smoke tobacco indoors but you are allowed to smoke cannabis so long as there's no tobacco in the joint. One irony is that the Netherlands is probably the only place where a proper debate was conducted on the issue of secondhand smoke and politicians concluded that there was insufficient evidence to justify a comprehensive ban.[12]

Instead the Dutch parliament opted to give restaurants and bars until 2009 to improve ventilation and air cleaning, together with more no-smoking areas (a compromise that I advocated in the Scottish Parliament). It was not to be, however, for a new government in The Hague acquiesced to the public health lobby and scrapped that sensible arrangement. How low can a low country get? Only a few smoking rooms will be able to meet the new requirements, but for how long? Cannabis was given a get-out as a sop to the right-on belief that that particular dead leaf is cool, and of course it's a big tourist attraction along with the canals and windmills.

In Germany the thought of a British or Irish style smoking ban doesn't seem to appeal. Again a compromise of sorts was reached whereby the federal (national) government delegated the authority to the lander (regional) governments resulting in a patchwork of outcomes, rather like the USA. Most regions allow premises to have smoking and non-smoking rooms and some clubs allow smoking which has led to many bars changing their status to retain their customers, an action recently given the backing of German courts. The fact that the last great crusade against smoking was run by a certain Herr Hitler does not make the forcible prosecution of the law any easier. I was recently able to enjoy a fine Partagas Series D P2 after my meal in a Berlin restaurant with a coffee and a brandy in a perfectly acceptable side room. As has often been the case since 1945, Germany comes out better than Britain, this time valuing more highly its freedom and tolerance that we helped to return to them but have given away for ourselves.

One point that Jackson noticed was how, across the world, nowhere is as addicted as the UK to those ever present 'No

Smoking' signs. In other countries the lack of an ashtray is enough to indicate a no smoking policy. In Britain we have to shout at people in large letters, defacing our buildings and our property. If you're a smoker it's hard to escape the bully state. It's there, around every corner, on every entrance, on every shop door. Even churches have had to erect a 'No Smoking' sign. When was the last time you saw someone smoke in a church?

Not at all countries are like Britain. At Zurich airport in Switzerland, Jackson noted with some surprise "half a dozen smoking lounges with shocking signs 'Smokers welcome!'" He dubbed Austria "a smoker's paradise". "In Vienna," he wrote, "one of the world's most beautiful and civilised cities, you can smoke everywhere, and there are wonderfully inviting tobacconists on practically every corner, too. We went to a lively pub/restaurant that brewed its own excellent beer, and although more than half the customers were smoking (cigars and pipes, too) the ventilation was good enough that the air wasn't smoky at all. My bassist, who doesn't like smoke, was amazed, but I can hardly blame him. One of the many facts persistently buried by the antis is that it really isn't difficult, with existing technology, to make tobacco smoke in the air barely noticeable."

Spain has what appears to a popular compromise. Bars and restaurants that are larger than 100 square metres have to provide separate smoking room if they want to accommodate smokers. Below that size the owners can decide for themselves whether they wish to be smoking or non-smoking establishments. Everyone has a choice: proprietors, customers and, most important, bar workers. (Needless to say this perfect arrangement is now under threat from the socialist government currently in power in Spain.)

Jackson concluded his smoker's guide to Europe in what he called the "most inhospitable country for smokers in the world". He wrote: "It's a country whose ban has absolutely no exceptions or exemptions, where outside smoking is mostly uncomfortable or impossible, where anti-smoking propaganda does not let up for a minute and where ugly signage blares at you from every angle. A country where anti-smokers are so arrogant and empowered that restrictions are proliferating in outside areas and even starting to reach into peoples' homes, and where, if you admit to being a smoker, you can lose your job or be refused medical treatment."[13]

Yes, Joe Jackson was back in Britain.

The hounding of smokers, the continual introduction of new restrictions, ever tighter regulations, the threat of fines and the use of CCTV to police people who consume a perfectly legal product is designed to make social pariahs out of law-abiding citizens. Eleven million adults choose to smoke. They have a vote too. They have a right to be tolerated, not demonised; accommodated not kicked out onto the street. If you don't smoke but enjoy drinking alcohol or eating what you want (not what the state wants you to eat) it's in your interest to support smokers in their battle against the bully state.

Notes:
1. When I write of the smoking bans in the British Isles I do, of course mean the ban on smoking in enclosed public places, not a ban on smoking in its entirety. To use the long-hand version every time – and it will be often – would be laborious for me and boring for the reader so I ask some forbearance in using the short-hand version, even though it is not literally accurate.
2. Scottish Press Association 2004
3. *The Times*, 22 July 2009
4. *Guardian*, 9 June 2004
5. *Daily Telegraph*, 10 June 2004
6. *The Times*, 25 July 2008
7. *The Times*, 15 June 2009
8. Dr Eamonn Butler, *The Times*, 25 July 2008
9. bmj.com, 30 August 2003
10. *Guardian*, 10 September 2009
11. Joe Jackson, *Stubbed out Down Under*, The Free Society, 16 July 2008
12. The House of Lords Economic Affairs Committee came to a similar conclusion in 2006 when it published a report on the management of risk.

The committee, whose members included former chancellor Lord Lawson, concluded that, "Passive smoking is an example in which [government] policy demonstrates a disproportionate response to a relatively minor health problem, with insufficient regard to statistical evidence."

13. Joe Jackson, *A Smoker's Guide to Europe and Beyond,* The Free Society, 7 & 8 April 2008

# Chapter Five

# BULLYING BILLY BUNTER

*"There was a time when food was just something you ate.*
*Now it's something you fear."*

## - RAB MCNEIL, THE SCOTSMAN

"Doctors can't decide on definition of obesity," shouted the newspaper headline. "Great," I thought, "I can eat another fish supper." Maybe I could also have some deep fried mushrooms too, better than those sickly deep fried Mars bars. (They're for the tourists. I don't know anyone in Scotland who eats them.) The nanny state has given up trying to cajole us to eat healthily and now tries to coerce us. When it comes to referring patients to weight loss clinics it appears that 25 per cent of doctors use that pesky body mass index (BMI) measure and medical history to decide. A further 40 per cent use only the BMI, and 25 per cent (my kind of doctor) don't bother with any measurements at all but instead take a considered judgment. The upshot of this is that there will no doubt be more guidelines, more regulations, for doctors to follow, matched by even more money being spent on advertisements and initiatives telling us to stop killing ourselves with kindness. Scotland ranks second only to the USA in some league tables on obesity, and yet Scots have never lived longer and there have never been so many people in gyms running at a standstill, rowing to nowhere and pushing up weights, rather than daisies.

But surely, as long as we pay for the consequences of our lifestyle choices ourselves, then whose business is it anyway, however it's measured? I don't just love a Big Mac or my Double Sausage Egg McMuffin. I love my Sugar Puffs, especially with Jersey milk. Was it the Honey Monster that did it for me? Well, er, no, because I've been eating Sugar Puffs since before the Honey Monster was a twinkle in some marketing chap's eye. I'm sure "It's G-r-r-r-eat" being Tony the Tiger, or Coco the Monkey or Snap Crackle and Pop, but they are figments of our inventive minds. They aren't real, or do some people put something stronger in their cereal bowls?

In 2008 Nigel Griffiths, Labour MP for South Edinburgh, decided to fight the obesity 'epidemic' by piloting a private members' bill through Westminster – the Food Products (Marketing to Children) Bill to be exact – hoping to cast Tony and his chums into Room 101. Supporters of the bill seemed to forget that Tony and other food mascots often promote active lifestyles, giving away footballs and encouraging kids to take up sport. In fact, cartoon characters used to promote so-called unhealthy foods do more for children's health than all those MPs who seem to have forgotten their own childhood. Let's not forget too that McDonald's, in the form of Ronald McDonald, have funded the training of 11,500 football coaches for kids in the last five years.

Tony the Tiger was born in 1952 when Kelloggs held a competition for a character to promote their sugar frosted flakes. He has been roaring his famous slogan on our tellys ever since. Other cereals from Kelloggs and rival food companies soon joined in employing the age-old advertising technique of using a fictional or real character, from a salty seaman to a cheeky chipmunk, to endorse a product and extol its virtues. From cartoon characters to real people, Gary Lineker is only the latest in a long line of celebrities to promote food in an entertaining way.

The Food Products (Marketing to Children) Bill was defeated but it will come back in another form. Alternatively the threat of legislation will be used to extract some sort of commitment from manufacturers to limit their budgets, tone down their advertising or put Tony into an old toons home. While the bill sought to ban the advertising of so-called 'unhealthy foods' until after the nine o'clock watershed and from child-centred websites altogether, many campaigners didn't think that went far enough. The Consumers' Association wanted a more robust approach including controls on the packaging as well. If campaigners had their way Tony would be consigned to the marketing history books.

Let's forget for the moment the fact that Frosties are a wonderfully tasty treat that encourages children to at least have something to eat before going to school. (When I was an MSP studying the evidence for or against having universal free school meals, a regular argument in favour of free lunches was how often kids went to school with no breakfast at all). Let us also put aside the fact that any food taken in moderation will not, in itself, make anyone obese, and let's ignore that the designation of what is a healthy or unhealthy is open to interpretation and abuse.

The question I have for MPs, consumer action groups and the breakfast bullies is simple enough: if the promotion of children's foods has been around since the Fifties, why was childhood obesity not a problem then? Is the answer that it is not the consumption of food such as Frosties and Sugar Puffs or the occasional Big Mac that is the issue, but the significant change in children's lifestyles that has led to many of them being less active? As a kid I walked four miles a day going to and from school. I played football after school, I clambered over hills in the neighbouring Queen's Park, I swam, I played hospital tig in the school playground, I played football after tea and I learned Scottish country dancing. I ate like a horse but I was thin.

Today I drive most places. I have stopped playing five-a-side football (gammy knee) and no longer sweat it out at the local disco. The result is I've gained weight. I recently took up swimming and try to book only those hotels that have a pool. I manage about three swimming sessions a week, seven when I'm working abroad, and I've lost 22lbs in the last year (eleven bags of sugar!). When my food and alcohol intake remain constant my weight fluctuates with my level of physical activity. Reduce the former and increase the latter and it begins to fall off.

Kids today are likely to be driven to school, the playing field has most likely been sold off for housing, the school playground is now a car park for teachers (and pupils if it's a secondary) and extra-curricular sports are unheard of. Tony the Tiger might as well be redrawn and renamed Sammy the Scapegoat. He and his friends are an easy target for politicians looking for the next notch on their truncheons. Instead they should wake up and smell their unfairtrade coffee. Blaming the marketing of popular foods is to ignore the decline in physical exercise and to absolve people from their own personal responsibilities. The logical extension would be to ban all advertising because every product carries some risk. Learning how to say no to their progeny is one of the most important tasks parents must learn. The joyless 'I know better than thee' approach will not reduce children's waistlines one inch.

Anyone who has witnessed Jamie Oliver's television exposé of British school dinners has reason to be concerned. Not because our children are being fed processed and reformed shapes of flavour-enhanced, deep fried, reheated pieces of meat that need preservatives, colourings, coatings, salts, gums and other gloopy additives before having smiley faces pressed into them to make them appetising. No, because they don't know any better.

One of the reasons why the nanny state is tolerated and is transforming effortlessly into the bully state is because we are being denied freedom of choice, especially informed choice, with the result that we are losing the ability to look after ourselves and our children. I have absolutely no doubt that many of the so-called problems that are said to confront people today exist not because we have too much liberty but because we have too little. Knowledge, they say, is power, and in relation to food few people have the knowledge they require to make an informed choice and so they rely on the state to make their decisions for them.

As a gourmand of some fame in my own small circle of friends one cannot help feeling embarrassment and disgust with much of the muck that is served up at some schools. For me, rather than despairing about the constant parade of pizzas, burgers and chips, not to mention the now demonised turkey twizzler, there was a far more shocking revelation. When Jamie Oliver held up a leek to a group of primary children and asked "Does anyone know what this is?", one solitary girl replied: "A potato?" So divorced was she from the origins of the food she ate that the poor soul didn't know her leeks from her potatoes and, I guess, doesn't know what her chips are made from either.

Jamie then showed the children some sticks of rhubarb, but there was no hope. You got the feeling they wouldn't have known custard if it was poured over them. For me, it was this complete detachment from food in its natural state that was so shocking. I was already aware that some kids don't realise where chicken drumsticks come from but to not know your common or garden vegetable or have tasted a fresh strawberry is extraordinary. And it's not the fault of the council-run dinner service. It's the fault of us, the parents. If we are going to enjoy and keep our freedoms we must accept more responsibility.

When I look back on my youth I can remember the tastes and aromas of the kitchen, the sawdust on the butcher's floor as the blood dripped off the carcasses; the fishmonger gutting the fish in front of you and the baker bringing the tray of hot pies out of the oven. The food wasn't just there to eat, you experienced it. Living near Holyrood in Edinburgh I saw sheep in the Queen's Park and perch in St Margaret's Loch, which my dad and I would poach before the parkies came on duty. My mum would gut the perch and we'd have them grilled for breakfast. Occasionally I'd be sent to the butchers to pick up a sheep's heid that would be boiled in a big pot for our spaniel to devour. Or maybe it would be tripe, which my mum would scrub (and I mean scrub!) before boiling it all day for my dad and I (she loathed it), served with potatoes, onions, some milk and ground white pepper. Wonderful!

With a family to cook for my mum baked a lot back then: cakes, malt loafs and Eve's puddings. The treat for me was mixing the ingredients and eating the leftovers in the bowl. Uncooked cake mix always tasted so good! I was allowed to peel potatoes and slice them for real chips or grate the carrots for lentil soup. This wasn't just fun. I could sneak the odd chip or carrot and eat them raw. Marvellous.

When I was three and four I used to be left at my grandma's while my parents worked. My grandad, an engineering inspector, was out working on the Forth Bridge but had nurtured a large garden full of raspberries, rhubarb, blackcurrants, gooseberries, strawberries, Brussels sprouts, potatoes, tomatoes, lettuce, beetroot and carrots. He also had six trees growing pears, apples and plums. I played hide and seek and built my own wee gang hut in the garden amongst it all I knew what all these delicacies of the Scottish soil tasted like, raw, and I respected the care and graft that my grandfather doled out in equal measure to grow these fruits of his garden.

I didn't really like mushrooms but I liked mushroom soup. Campbell's Condensed Cream of Mushroom Soup, to be exact. Then, long before Chicken Tonight, my mum told me that if you didn't add the water you could use the condensed liquid as a sauce for chicken. I then added extra mushrooms and eventually graduated by dumping the Campbell's soup and making buttered mushrooms with garlic on toast, mushrooms over my steak, and then to-die-for honey-glazed button mushrooms with sesame seeds. So much for not liking mushrooms! When I became a teenager I regularly cooked the occasional tea. Nothing fancy. I was yet to discover French or Indian food, but I began to discover lots of vegetables as well as different meats and the various ways to cook them. Now I'm rarely out of the kitchen, or other people's kitchens, given half the chance.

But that was a generation ago and lifestyles have changed. It's not just that more convenience foods are available or home delivery meals are a phone call away. We also try and cram more activities into our lives so we rarely cook for our children or involve them with the food they eat. So let's not rush to attack our schools or the dinner ladies. When I was at school our please for chips always fell on deaf ears; the same with burgers or anything that wasn't plain fare. There were no sandwich shops, fast food eateries, delis, and the like, able to cater for kids at lunchtime, so we just put up with it. Still, I loved my school grub and was known to go to two sittings on some days. Today the only way to entice kids into the school canteen is to give them chips with everything, often served up with grated cheese. (A burger is considered a banquet!) The dinner ladies are in an invidious position. Serve 'real' food and it often gets wasted. Serve piping-hot processed pap and some kids might do you the favour of eating it. So we should get off our high horse and instead of lambasting them for responding to the market demands of their customers we should own up and realise that it's us, the parents, who are the problem and we should resolve it ourselves, not wait for the state to bully us into action.

As parents let's ask if we could do things better, could we do things differently? I hold up my hand and say, yes, I could. I love cooking so much I just got on and did it without letting my sons so much as peel and slice an onion. Watching the parents in Jamie Oliver's show I sensed that they had been seduced by the instant gratification of our consumer society. They needed as much help as the kids. Unless we as parents bring our children into the kitchen, let them dice a turnip, shred a cabbage or boil a beetroot we have only ourselves to blame if they reject the ratatouille or body swerve the broccoli while at school.

That's not to say that the occasional sausage roll, haggis pudding or beefburger is a bad thing, they're not. The point about eating well is to enjoy the variety, reflecting the seasons, the weather and the cooks' variable skills. Parents need help but neither they nor their children need to be nannied or bullied. They just need to be able to understand that most basic of things, the food they eat to survive, and how to make it desirable and edible. Banning some foods, putting health warnings on others, and restricting children from having choices compounds the problem because it takes away the responsibility of making a choice, learning from mistakes and discovering what works. In his attempts to ban some foods Jamie Oliver took on the role of nanny, which was unfortunate. He should have sought out young mums and focussed on them rather than criticising the dinner ladies and food manufacturers.

Of course it was no coincidence that no sooner had the Scottish Parliament banned smoking in pubs and even 'public' places such as private clubs, it moved to ban something else, the humble mutton pie.[1] As the former honorary president of the Parliamentary Pie Club and a guest judge at the World Pie Championships I would feel a sense of loss if I hadn't had a good juicy mutton pie, sometimes with curried beans, sometimes with chips, but usually on its own once a week. Made properly, the Scotch pie is a culinary triumph. It is Scotland's original fast food, an ideal meal on the move. Although it is sacrilege to some, it has been adapted successfully into chicken curry pies, haggis-neeps-and-tattie pies, macaroni cheese pies or even more adventurous or outrageous pies such as lamb and mint or turkey, chipolata and cranberry!

Just thinking about the original combination of the light but crisp pastry shell, the seasoned succulent minced meat and the moistness of the mutton's juices makes my mouth water. But much as I love pies I can't recall eating them every day of my life, or ever wanting to. Like most folk I like a choice and will only have a pie when I feel like it or it is the handiest nosh to nab as I hurtle about in my busy life.

But no, the parliamentary powers that be decided that to protect me and other MSPs from ourselves there should be no pies available in the Scottish Parliament on Monday and Friday. I and others who might have forgotten their Tibetan yoghurt, or were just famished, were denied the choice. It would have to be something trendy and 'good' for you; a quiche (a scrambled egg pie cross-dressing in short crust pastry) or a chickpea and sunflower seed salad, perhaps. I don't know, I didn't hang around to find out. Like many others I simply took my custom elsewhere, to the chippy a hundred yards up the road that sold really healthy stuff like deep fried Mars bars. (I chose the haggis supper with Edinburgh's own runny brown sauce.) Embarrassed by the reaction of even the most lily-livered do-gooding parliamentarians, the ban was officially denied and explained as a matter of "supply and demand". That's spin doctor speak for "You can demand it but we won't supply it"! The Parliament that began by banning fox hunting and saw more foxes killed, and went on to ban smoking in pubs so more people would smoke at home, had now chosen to ban the mutton pie so we all ended up having a chippy (or going to the pub for a liquid lunch)! That's the bully state for you.

Pub food is another target. Not satisfied with banning the pipe, the fag and the half-corona from Scottish pubs, the avaricious eyes of social planners have thought of introducing restrictions on pub grub through the licensing laws. Funny, I don't remember that being debated when the Licensing Bill went through Parliament. Forget your humble mutton pie or bangers and mash and face a future of soya bean curd and cos lettuce with a low fat dressing. Since the Scottish Nationalists came to power the idea seems to have melted away like an arctic roll on a summer's day. (Maybe Alex Salmond likes his pies?) But like all these ideas it will be revived, once there is some 'research' published to show that pub grub is the cause of cancer of the colon or some such illness.

Ice cream is on the radar too, with ice-cream vans facing a ban from outside schools in Dunbartonshire. Ice cream vendors up and down the land face meltdown as the craze to remove anything pleasurable from our lives gains momentum. If the all-knowing all-seeing bureaucrats get their way the world won't end with a banger or a Whippy. We're all going to live forever.

The obesity 'epidemic' is of course used for all sorts of needless government interventions. What would we do without government? It's so reassuring to know that no stone is left unturned and that every care is taken to ensure we won't do silly things that are bad for us. Figures from official government research is used to tell us that obesity is an epidemic that will become the biggest single cause of deaths or illness in 20 years time. So government intervened and secured a deal with food manufacturers. Those king size Mars bars, Snickers and the like were to be downsized and vending machines removed from schools.

What a futile gesture, what an abdication of responsibility. The rise in obesity is a genuine health concern and it is understandable that strategists in the NHS want to plan for its effects, but it's not an epidemic because it's not a disease. In science words have specific meanings but politicians and political health campaigners blur those meanings by using words such as 'epidemic' and 'disease' as if they mean the same thing. They don't. Obesity is a risk factor but it is not itself a disease, just as having a family history of prostate cancer is not the same as having prostate cancer. For all but a very small minority with glandular or metabolic problems, obesity is a symptom of lifestyle choices. Even then, until recently, when I went round schools every week I strained my eyes to find the large number of fatties that I was being told existed. The vast majority of kids looked pretty normal to me. Reducing the size of chocolate bars won't change anything. Indeed I would argue that if there is a problem it's the smaller fun-size bars because they encourage people to snack throughout the day and instead of being satisfied by a full-size bar they are left wanting more. But that's their choice and I wouldn't outlaw either size. If we want to change our body profiles we have to change our lifestyles and that's up to us. It's the responsibility of the individual not the government.

Now, if our caring rulers were to ensure that all our schools provided enough exercise through dancing, team sports and PE that would make a difference. More important, if kids could be allowed to be kids and play games in the playground, running around chasing each other, playing tig, hospital tig (my favourite), British bulldog or even football or dodgy, that would really help. But to many state nannies these activities are a health and safety risk or they encourage elitism, favouritism or, would you believe it, bullying so they are discouraged or banned. The truth is that most politicians pay lip service to exercise in schools, turning up for photo calls before being driven off in a ministerial limousine. The many attempts that I and others like Margo MacDonald, a fellow MSP, made to establish more PE time and more PE teachers were regularly ignored.

There is also a debate about whether or not obesity is a form of child neglect and councils should have the power to intervene to save children from their parents who leave them to eat mountains of food. The Local Government Association has suggested just such action to protect "dangerously overweight children". According to one LGA spokesman: "Councils are increasingly having to consider taking action where parents are putting children's health in real danger. Councils would step in to deal with an undernourished or neglected child, so should a case with a morbidly obese child be different? It is vital that councils, primary care trusts and the NHS work with parents to ensure children don't end up dangerously overweight in the first place."

They have a point. If parents place children at risk through bad diet and lack of exercise, is it not right for a council to keep the child's health under review? Well, given the depth of evidence that children placed in care are far more likely to end up in a life of crime, drug addiction and sexual abuse, it would have to be a very serious threat to a child's life before social workers are able to present a case to a court, equating a child being allowed by parents to eat too much, with parents leaving a child to starve. There have been a very few cases of morbidly obese children but one does not have to think long and hard before realising that the line of where such parental rights could be over-ruled would become hazy and some councils would try to extend their 'concern' to children who are merely overweight, arguing that they are the children most likely to progress to seriously or morbidly obese and they have to be 'protected' from their parents.

Unfortunately councils have a bad habit of trying to extend their powers and it wouldn't be long before such interventions began to encroach into family life. One can easily see parents being told to enrol their children in fat camps, with a refusal counting as a black mark against the parents. Too many refusals or a combination of other recalcitrant behaviour and the child could be taken away from their parents and into council care. I would be content to leave decisions such as these to the courts, under very strict criteria, rather than at the discretion of politicians or their officials.

Just as I was finishing the manuscript for this book the *Daily Telegraph* published a report that claimed that the Labour government has a "secret plan to send children to NHS fat camps". According to the paper, "Primary school pupils identified as being overweight will automatically be offered a place on a state-funded diet and exercise scheme. Although parents will have the right to refuse to send their children to the classes, ministers hope the majority will attend … Margaret Morrissey, founder of family lobby group Parents Outloud, said it was "unforgivable" to promote schemes which would inevitably encourage humiliation to be heaped on those children bused off to fat camps. She said: "This has gone beyond a nanny state, beyond Big Brother. To label young children as overweight because they are carrying a few extra pounds makes them so vulnerable to bullying, and increases the risk of developing eating disorders, especially among the girls. Obviously it is unfortunate if parents feed their children badly but this Government appears to have forgotten that we do not live in a dictatorship." [2]

This is all especially ironic as it is often other council bullies, in one guise or another, who go around telling children they can't run around or chase each other in the playground as someone might trip and get hurt; that ball games aren't allowed just in case a window is broken (and somebody gets hurt); or they can't play team games as the losers might get psychologically (as well as physically) hurt! Is it any wonder that children lack exercise that would help burn off all that excess fat?

In Queensland, Australia, in 2008 the state premier Anna Bligh released a discussion paper suggesting restrictions on fast food advertising to tackle childhood obesity (citing her own parental experience of "pester-power" as a justification) while at the same time supporting a local school that stopped children doing physical exercise such as cartwheels and handstands in the playground. "I support [school] principals making decisions to keep children safe," she told the media.[3]

In the same year in Scotland NHS Tayside health board banned sugary drinks in vending machines at some of its hospitals with the support of the British Dental Health Foundation (BDHF) and the Scottish Government which urged other health boards to follow suit. BDHF chief executive Nigel Carter said: "The foundation not only backs the NHS Tayside decision, but calls for a UK-wide ban on sugar drinks and snacks in hospitals, surgeries and health centres." The Foundation wants the NHS to fill its vending machines with water, fruit juices and 'healthy' snacks.

In England a Department of Health spokesman said: "We have stated in the new obesity strategy that we expect the public sector to lead by example." As one blogger on the BBC website shrewdly observed: "If I'm having emergency surgery at 3.00am and the surgeon feels he/she needs a Mars bar and a can of coke I want him/her to have Mars bar and a can of Coke. And more importantly, patients are generally in hospital because they are already sick, probably feeling miserable. Why should we deny them a bit of 'junk' food if it makes them feel better?"[4]

The fight to control our eating habits is not just a battle against us, the consumer, but between cities, local authorities and even countries. Such is the zealotry of the public health campaigners that they actually vie to be the first to ban something and are hugely disappointed when they are beaten to the punch. In December 2006 the New York City Board of Health voted to ban the use of trans fats in city restaurants and Chicago was aggrieved to not have introduced the ban first! A Chicago alderman who was pushing for similar regulations in his own city, reportedly told the *New York Times*, "I'm disappointed we're losing bragging rights to be the first city in the nation to do this."[5]

(When Ireland introduced its public smoking ban in 2004 I was struck by the way that politicians and campaigners in Ireland congratulated themselves on becoming the first country in the world to introduce such a comprehensive piece of legislation. Two years later their counterparts in Scotland revelled in the fact that Scotland was the first nation in the United Kingdom to ban smoking in every pub and club. Then, just as I was completing this book, the British Medical Association called on Britain to become the first country in the world to introduce a comprehensive ban on alcohol advertising, sponsorship and promotions.[6] It's as if banning things, in the eyes of health campaigners, has become a symbol of a town or country's virility.)

What happened in New York with trans fats was a typical piece of nanny state regulation. Trans fats were introduced by food processors and restaurants to replace saturated fats, which are generally considered to be bad for one's health. They did this without legal intervention but as a market response to customer concerns and the advantages gained from marketing healthier products. So in baked goods, fried foods, salad dressings, margarine and other foods, trans fats were introduced with the advantage of a longer shelf life than other alternatives, thus keeping costs down. Alarm began to mount when research suggested that trans fats raise levels of a particularly unhealthy form of cholesterol that has been linked to heart disease. As a result a number of large chain restaurants started to withdraw their use. Not satisfied with this perfectly reasonable, self-regulating behaviour that gave people the choice of whether to eat at restaurants that used trans fats, the New York authorities stepped in and banned oils, margarines and shortening from recipes that contained more than a half-gram of trans fat per serving. By 1 July 2008 large chain restaurants had to remove all menu items that exceeded the limit, including bread, cakes, chips and salad dressings.

New York's trans fat regulations are enforced by health department restaurant inspectors who can issue fines of at least $200. They check the packaging of ingredients used in restaurants for the amount of trans fats they contain and then calculate how much is used in each serving, but prepared food is not routinely tested. Chefs and restaurateurs argue that the taste of their culinary creations is affected and that it is hard to replicate the taste and texture of some items without trans fats. Health activists deny this, arguing that alternatives are available.

Not content with the trans fat regulations which, because of the negative reaction from restaurateurs, received all the media coverage, the New York authorities displayed their real nannying streak by slipping through another by-law that required certain restaurants to display prominently the calorie content of each item on menu boards or near cash registers. Health officials justified their action as a response to what they argued is a nationwide obesity epidemic. Health officials estimated that about ten percent of the city's restaurants, mainly large chains that have highly standardised menus and portions, would be affected.[7]

Such initiatives may not be the end of the world but it is typical of how we are constantly being pointed, ushered, moved and shepherded or 'nudged' in the direction of our masters' choosing. The fact that food manufacturers and restaurants have been moving to inform the consumer more and more and in ever greater detail is never enough. Compulsion is now the order of the day.

What effect does calorie information have? *The Economist* reported how one study found that when the information was prominently displayed in fast food chains customers ordered foods with an average of 52 fewer calories, but another discovered, bizarrely, that diners ordered lower calorie meals only on Mondays and Tuesdays![8] I've no problem with fast food chains displaying this information if they want to. I just don't see the need for laws to enforce it, not least because it creates more red tape and bureaucracy.

McDonald's reduced the standard portion of French fries, cutting not only the number of calories but also its costs. Le Pain Quotidien, a bakery chain with 17 outlets in New York and $165m in worldwide sales, has seen business improve in the metropolis after revising its menu, cutting portions and eliminating items with lots of calories. Le Pain Quotidien is considering rolling out the same information voluntarily in Los Angeles and Washington DC even though there are no laws requiring it to do so. Starbucks, meanwhile, changed its regular milk from whole fat to semi-skimmed, reducing by 14 per cent the calories in its drinks. (Low-fat milk just happens to be cheaper, coincidentally.)

Interestingly, a study carried out at Subway, which already markets a range of foods for their low calorie or healthy appeal, found that "there was no significant difference in mean calories purchased by patrons reporting seeing but not using calorie information and patrons who reported not seeing calorie information".[9] So why bother imposing this information on us? There is clearly a legitimate role in public health to police hygiene issues but when it comes to health and safety in foods the authorities don't know where to draw the line and their regime is pernicious in the way it operates.

There can be few people in Britain who don't like Chinese food, such are the vast number of Chinese restaurants and takeaways. One of the most popular Chinese dishes in Britain is Peking duck, that crispy form of delicious tasty duck served with cucumber and spring onion, with small thin pancakes and hoi-sin sauce. The duck is cooked in a special way, with air blown between the skin and the meat before it is roasted in special Chinese ovens, 6ft-tall drum-shaped appliances that can roast up to 24 ducks and four suckling pigs at a time, much larger than a conventional commercial oven. They are heated via a central burner at the base so the heat can rise up through the hanging racks of specially treated ducks and reach temperatures of 300oC. Many Chinese restaurants get their duck from Chinese supermarkets or from other restaurants that have taken the trouble to invest in special Chinese ovens imported from the Far East. Now, however, health and safety officers at Westminster City Council have discovered that many of these special ovens do not have an EU approved rating, a 'CE' stamp, to show they have met strict and rigorous standards.

Here's what happened. At a routine inspection of a Chinese restaurant in May 2008 it was noted that the specially imported oven did not have a 'CE' marking. The wheels of the health and safety juggernaut began to turn. A council spokesman said: "If the restaurants want to continue cooking ducks in the traditional manner they will need to get new ovens which will comply with EU standards by having CE marking. We are absolutely not picking on the Chinese community. This is an issue with any kind of ethnic type of food where they may well be using catering equipment imported from outside the EU. We are not aware of a single injury or accident involving these duck ovens but now we are aware of this issue we want to prevent any accidents happening."[10] This, by the way, was the same council that in 2006 went round Korean restaurants confiscating table-top 'dish-warmers' that did not meet European safety standards. Westminster Council officials admitted there had been no reports of health problems associated with the special ovens which is hardly surprising because commercial kitchens are one of the most highly regulated work areas in Britain today. If there was a problem with any of these ovens it would surely have come to light before.

Nevertheless council inspectors decided to visit Chinese restaurants that use the ovens, sealing them up with tape if they not carry a CE or 'Conformité Européenne' certifying mark. At least ten London restaurants, including some in the famous Chinatown district of Soho, were affected. Even the famous £40-a-head Phoenix Palace in Marylebone, a Chinese restaurant patronised by Tony and Cherie Blair, Gordon Brown, foreign secretary David Miliband and deputy leader Harriet Harman, couldn't escape the inspectors' purge. The restaurant had imported its oven from China eight years previously because none were manufactured in Europe. Yet it had to order a new one costing £4,000. To say the Chinese were offended would be an understatement. Don't take my word for it. This is what Chinese celebrity chef Ken Hom had to say: "It's absurd. What do the Europeans know about making Chinese duck? It's just as outrageous as people in Hong Kong being told they can't make fish and chips. I am livid." [11]

There are times when even the most ardent supporters of greater European integration must wince, times when they pick up their morning newspaper and literally choke on their euroflakes as they read about yet another attempt to homogenise our lives, just like the dairy milk now splattered over their front page headlines. In an attempt to protect Europeans from suffering from food poisoning after eating steak tartare, the euro bullies now insist that meat cannot be allowed to hang for longer than they decree. While the EU elites were busy conspiring to prevent ordinary mortals from having a say in how we are governed by denying us a referendum on the new European constitution, they still found time to ensure that mince cannot come from beef that has been hung for longer than five days. Given that British meat is regularly hung for anything between 14-28 days to impart more flavour, the impact will be to drive up prices through greater wastage, and give us less tasty mince into the bargain.

Clearly these so-called food experts know nothing about steak tartare. As a dish that is made from raw steak, a raw egg yolk, onions, capers and chillies, and served cold and uncooked, it is not the meat that it is likely to cause an upset tummy but the egg! Beef eaten raw can, very occasionally, cause tapeworm in humans if the eggs of the tapeworm exist in the meat and are not killed by the cooking process. Hanging meat for a shorter time does nothing to prevent or reduce this risk. Similarly there is no evidence that hanging meat for a few days less makes any significant difference to the number of bacteria contained in the meat, or their potency. Far more important is the temperature that the meat is stored at than the days it is hung. Don't just take my word for it, the food hygiene expert Professor Hugh Pennington has argued this point himself.[12]

Like so many before it, this latest regulation is uncalled for, unnecessary and unfair. By pretending to protect people from the risks of eating steak tartare (a very, very small minority) everyone who eats cottage pie, lasagne, spaghetti bolognese, curried mince, steak mince pies or good old-fashioned mince and tatties is going to be inconvenienced and have to pay more into the bargain. It is all so unnecessary. Anyone who eats steak tartare should, and usually does, know the risk. Like tripe, it's an acquired taste. It is often made by the waiter, or chef, right in front of you and then served. No-one can be in any doubt about what they are about to eat. And it's their choice!

Britain normally consumes about 135,000 tons of fresh minced beef and another 350,000 tons of mince in prepared foods, including pies, sausages and ready-made meals. As mince is made normally from the leftovers of butchered meat, the new rules will now require butchers to earmark a whole animal only for mince, or they will have to butcher the animal earlier because any leftovers from animals hung for more than five days cannot be available for mince. All these interventions will drive the price up, with butchers predicting an increase of 40p a pound being added to the average price of £1.50 a pound.[13]

The attacks on our eating habits will no doubt continue. No culinary tradition, no cultural cuisine, good or bad, will be spared. As we are about to see, our drinking habits are under attack too.

Notes:

1.  Also known as a Scotch pie, a shell pie or, in Dundee, a 'peh'
2.  *Daily Telegraph*, 6 September 2009
3.  goldcoast.com.au, 27 August 2008
4.  BBC News, 10 October 2008
5.  *New York Times*, 6 December 2006
6.  *Daily Telegraph*, 9 September 2009
7.  *New York Times*, 6 December 2006
8.  *The Economist*, 28 August 2008
9.  Openmarket.org, 30 August 2008
10. *Daily Mail*, 19 July 2008
11. *Daily Record*, 25 March 2008
12. Cooking beef to 56oC, identified by it no longer being pink, or freezing it to -5oC will kill the tapeworm larvae
13. Since writing the price has indeed climbed to £1.99 per pound (Tesco, 31 August 2009)

# Chapter Six

# A BINGE OF BULLYING

*'The point to remember is that what the government gives it must first take away.'*

– JOHN S. COLEMAN

Happy hours? I plead guilty. I've actually gone to a pub during a happy hour (there, I've admitted it) and I can't even offer ignorance or naiveté as an excuse. I knew the pub in question had a happy hour and we chose it intentionally. It was when I worked in an office and a colleague's leaving party beckoned so the chance of cheap drinks was irresistible.

Pint after pint came in my direction as I racked up six jars of Guinness and it only took three rounds to do it because it was a two for one offer between five and eight o'clock. (One of the golden rules of happy hours is that they always last more than an hour!) Then came the shock to my system. The happy hour was over and the drinks were at full price. Ouch! Fortunately I still had two pints of Guinness left to drink and I was in no rush. And that's my point. The pace of my drinking hadn't changed (four pints over three hours), I'd simply saved money. Do happy hours distort people's behaviour? Do they make binge drinkers of all of us? I don't think so.

Frankly I think it's a myth that has been cooked up by the usual alliance of puritans, control freaks and prohibitionists. Sure, some people hit the happy hour and down their drinks quickly, getting wrecked in the process. Some go on to get into fights or fall asleep in their own vomit. Hopefully they'll learn. My guess, however, is that these are the same people who play daft drinking games such as Hancock's Half Hour. That's the one where every person in the group buys a round of spirits, but a different spirit, the aim being to down them in one and complete the task in half an hour. They're the same people who take weird drinks in test tubes that have nothing to do with the craft of brewing and distilling but everything to do with the chemistry of getting drunk, and as quickly as possible.

Happy hours exist however not to get us drunk, nor to force us to drink more quickly. They're there to attract customers to a bar so we get settled and stay for most of the night, or they exist to entice us to new bars or introduce us to new drinks. The people who make fools of themselves or cause trouble, sometimes violent trouble, don't need happy hours to get tanked up. Remove happy hours and the majority who don't abuse the concept become the victims while the guilty find other ways to wreak havoc. Whatever it is, they'll find a way because binging is about getting drunk, not about saving money.

If there's one thing that is stupid it's the idea that getting drunk is a sign of adulthood. It's not that way in Spain or France where getting plastered is commonly seen as a lack of self-control. That means we need to accompany drink with food more often. We need to learn to pace ourselves and we need to make it less of a forbidden fruit to our offspring. Banning happy hours is neither desirable nor practicable. What is needed is not a government-enforced change in publicans' pricing policies but a change in our drinking culture. Trying to fix the prices won't cure the hangover.

The campaign to change or control our drinking habits mirrors the war on tobacco. Increasingly we are subjected to calls for greater controls on our alcoholic intake, be it more restrictions on how and when we can buy alcohol, how much, the price, the packaging, the warnings – same old, same old. The same tactics that have been used in tobacco control are now advocated for alcohol consumption. (As I was completing this book the British Medical Association announced that it wants the government to ban alcohol advertising, sponsorship and promotions. The ban, says the BMA, should include all sports and music sponsorship, adverts in all media and an end to 'happy hour' and 'two-for-one' promotions. The BMA also called for a series of other measures including minimum pricing, an increase in taxation above the rate of inflation and to link the level to the alcoholic strength of the drink, reduce licensing hours in both off licences and pubs, and to force the drinks industry to pay for independent public health promotion.)[1]

Meanwhile … "Sorry, Jenny, you can't taste your mum's Mateus Rose, and hard luck, Johnny, you can't sip the froth off my pint of Boddingtons. The government won't allow me. You'll have to wait until you're 18 when, if you're lucky, I can still take you down to the local pub and it's up to the landlord to decide how much we drink." This farcical but entirely predictable conversation, where parents have been relieved of all responsibility for teaching their children how to consume alcohol safely, is just around the corner. That's the way we are heading after the government announced yet another review of guidelines as a prelude to a crackdown on so-called 'binge drinking'. If it was a crackdown on sweeping generalisations and junk science I'd be raising a glass to it but that would be illiberal of me so I had better resist the temptation.

Currently any child aged five or over is legally allowed to try alcohol at home under their parents' supervision. Measures likely to be considered in the future include raising the age at which children can legally be given alcohol by their parents, further restrictions on the advertising of alcohol (see above), more laws to stop teenagers drinking in public spaces (including prosecuting their parents if they do), tougher rules for bars and off licences that sell alcoholic drinks to under-age children, additional education in schools, plus higher taxes on low cost alcohol. All this despite the fact that the government's own figures show that the number of eleven to 15-year-olds taking alcohol regularly had dropped from a quarter to a fifth between 2001 and 2006.[2]

The forthcoming ban on brands of alcohol appearing on replica football strips is another example of how the state believes it has to force us all to behave better, despite the fact that the vast majority remain law-abiding, well mannered and, yes, sober members of society. As a parent of two boys now in their early twenties let me provide some simple observations. Kids demand football strips with 'Carlsberg' or 'Carling' emblazoned across the chest because they want the authentic strips their heroes wear, not some brandless imitation. Did it make my sons want to drink Carlsberg or Carling Black Label? No, they prefer real ale!

I believe that people who believe this sort of prohibition works are the same control freaks who want to remove Tony the Tiger from packets of Frosties. I also believe that restrictions on popular drinks such as alcopops or drinking outside in public areas can result in kids switching to stronger drinks and imbibing out of sight of anyone, a far more dangerous situation. Making alcohol difficult for our youth to obtain simply criminalises more people who break the law to buy it for their friends or siblings. And can I point out that 'more and better' sex education in schools with less parental responsibility has been accompanied by an explosion of under age sex, abortions and sexually transmitted disease and is then followed by demands for more sex education at an ever earlier age. I'm all for education but I return to my argument that it's best handled by parents and with a balance about responsibilities as well as rights.

When it comes to the cost of alcohol there is much less drunkenness and loutish behaviour in countries such as Spain where duty-paid alcohol is cheaper than duty-free drink in the UK. Changing our cultural behaviour cannot be done by introducing restriction after restriction, especially in a society where the state absolves people of so much of their own responsibility for themselves and their families and has worked tirelessly to see that there is no shame in behaving badly. After all, it's society's fault, not Johnny or Jenny's.[3]

The trend is clear. Having learned nothing about the futility of trying to change our social behaviour through the introduction of more and more laws like the smoking ban and restrictions on tobacco, the politicians and their puritanical functionaries are trying to bully us all over again, this time to conform to their ideal view of mirthless sobriety. A favourite tactic is scaremongering. Last year, for example, a report in the *British Medical Journal* said that binge drinking has increased to such an extent that cases of "exploding bladders" are on the rise in the UK. I kid you not. There seems to be only three documented cases in the entire world but a spokesman went on to say that "this new development certainly highlights the facts that the risks of heavy drinking go way beyond liver cirrhosis". Exploding imaginations more like.

In Scotland, where the licensing laws are different to England, drinking habits have changed beyond recognition in the last 30 years. It may be hard to believe now but there was a time when Edinburgh had few restaurants of any note and to get a drink after ten o'clock at night was nigh impossible unless you went to a club with sticky carpets and ordered chicken in a basket first. Edinburgh wasn't bohemian, it was backwater central. The only time it woke up was when the International Festival of the Arts and the accompanying Fringe injected a much-needed joie de vivre. The cold Forth winds and the dour Calvinist approach to drink and frolicking, together with a certain middle-class prurience, made Edinburgh the most unlikely place to come for a good time.

Unless you were a sailor, that is. Edinburgh's port of Leith and some notable redoubts in Stockbridge and Greenside offered solace of another kind. But it was the pressure from the Fringe, with its shows running into the wee sma' hours of the morning, that led to the city fathers relaxing the drinking laws with licensing extensions until one or two in the morning. Soon it was noticed that there really wasn't the trouble that some ever so dry curmudgeons had warned us about. People had a good time, they paced their drinking and they went home in relatively good order. Edinburgh's auld pubs were full of character. They reeked of smoke, cheap perfume and smelly toilets. The beer was Younger's Tartan Special, marketed with great irony by an Englishman (played by an Irishman) declaring "Your beer is good!" The wine was always Hirondelle, and the posher pubs sold Lutomer Laski Riesling or Bull's Blood. Drinking late was fun but it was not for the discerning or the faint-hearted.

Then it all changed. In 1976 the government, having noted Edinburgh's experience, liberalised the licensing laws across the whole of Scotland and allowed pubs to stay open until eleven o'clock with extensions until later relatively easy to acquire. Pubs could open on Sundays and 'all day' licences allowed drinking throughout the afternoon. Further liberalisation arrived in the Eighties and more relaxed, almost continental, hours followed, especially in Edinburgh where it was felt that the growing international flavour could support all night drinking if one knew which bars to move on to. Scotland was now more liberal than England.

It remained true however that many pubs and bars were pretty uncouth places. It wasn't noticed at the time but thanks to Margaret Thatcher's revival of the British economy, people, especially young people, had more disposable income (28 per cent over the period to be exact) and they used it not only to buy a home but to get out and have a good time. Economists might argue that good drove out bad. Ordinary folk would say that competition had arrived and with the help of a new breed of entrepreneur Edinburgh's (indeed Scotland's) drinking dens found themselves being challenged by stylish cocktail bars, wine bars, clubs and exclusive restaurants. Eating out, in particular, became the new sex.

It was long overdue but it was timely and the Edinburgh public, who had to support the new venues outside the four weeks of the Festival, lapped it up. Offered short city breaks, Hogmanay celebrations and spring sojourns, the tourists arrived in their droves.

The market grew and grew and the way to make a bar work was to raise its standards, not play to the lowest common denominator. Some bars couldn't keep pace and either closed down or enjoyed refits and refurbishments. Old shops, cinemas and banks (especially banks, with their wonderfully rich interiors of cornices and columns) were also revived. Competition drove standards up.

Then came the backlash. Some of the publicans losing custom didn't like what was happening and complained. Sure, there were more people drawn to the city centre, drunks might make mugs of themselves and there could be fights for that rare thing called a taxi. It always struck me, though, that the answer to this was to increase the number of taxis (a restriction defended by taxi drivers) and use the increased tax revenues to employ more police to discourage against any over-indulgence. The last thing Edinburgh needed was to control the number of pubs because doing that only protected the poorer, more threatening establishments from market forces. Sadly Edinburgh eventually took a wrong turning and in the new anti-alcohol consensus the city decided to use its licensing powers to limit the number of bars and black cabs in the city.

Overnight mediocrity was rewarded. Stinking toilets were preserved and investing in new premises became a gamble, if not impossible. In 2007 investors planning to deliver Hotel du Vin, a top-notch hotel, to the downmarket Forest Road were told they couldn't have a licence because there were too many bars already. (Fortunately this decision was reversed at a later meeting.) Licences should never be used to control numbers. The market does that. Licensing should be about setting minimum standards. To qualify for a licence investment should go into better restrooms, better décor and seating. Restrictions on investment in new bars only encourages more loutish behaviour because better facilities have the reverse effect, just like seating in football stadia has resulted in less violence.

In Scotland the Scottish Nationalist minority government (kept in power by two Greens, an independent and seventeen Conservative MSPs) is keen to introduce new restrictions on the purchase of alcohol, all in the name of reducing the nation's overall intake and especially targeting the young, citing incidents of alcohol-related crime as the reason. In particular the SNP government wants to stop 18 to 20-year-olds being able to buy alcohol in an off licence. The idea is primarily to stop over-18s buying alcohol for underage drinkers. Other measures being considered include separate aisles for alcohol sales in shops, a ban on drink promotions such as 'three-for-two' offers, a social responsibility levy, charging retailers for some of the damage done by drunks, curbs on advertising and setting a minimum price for alcoholic drinks

The Scottish government points to statistics related to alcohol consumption that would concern anyone who studied them. Over the last decade Scottish hospitals have seen an increase in alcohol-related admissions of almost 50 per cent whilst over half of Scottish prisoners in 2007 said they were drunk at the time of the offence. Some 40,000 hospital admissions a year and 70 per cent of assaults are alcohol-related, according to ministers.

Nevertheless the SNP's attempt to restrict off licence sales was defeated by combined opposition forces following a Conservative motion at the Holyrood parliament. Tory leader Annabel Goldie attacked "the ludicrous plans to criminalise a responsible, 20-year-old adult who wants to buy a bottle of wine to take home and celebrate the birth of his baby."[4] Others spoke out too. The Association of Chief Police Officers Scotland (ACPOS) warned that the policy would discriminate against law-abiding citizens. Bill Skelly, temporary deputy chief constable of Lothian and Borders Police and chairman of the ACPOS Licensing Sub-Group, warned that the plan was too simplistic, saying: "Those in the armed forces and emergency services who are respectively charged with the defence of our country and serving the needs of our communities would be excluded from purchasing alcohol. This proposal risks demonising and alienating perfectly law-abiding 18 to 20-year-olds. That cannot be right."[5] Chief inspector Micky Collins, from Dumfries and Galloway Constabulary, said: "Do we really want to prevent a 19-

year-old from buying a whisky gift-pack for his dad's birthday? The bigger problem we have is underage drinking at the moment."[6]

One absurdity raised by the Scottish Police Service was that licencees could be as young as 18. Its submission argued: "You could have someone running an off-sales premises, with all the concomitant responsibilities, but who could not himself purchase any alcohol from his, or any other, off-sales premises." Mad or what? Likewise a 20-year-old could go to a pub, drink ten pints of lager and then go to a supermarket and be refused a miniature of brandy for cooking with because of his or her age. Visit Scotland, the tourism quango charged with attracting travellers to the nation, pointed out that plans to stop off licences from offering free samples could prevent distilleries offering free drams for sampling at the end of distillery tours, hurting Scotland's vital tourist industry.

Studies in countries that have outlawed alcohol sales to anyone under 21 suggest that binge drinking among the young remains high. In the USA, where a debate is taking place in many states about relaxing the 21 and over rule for alcohol, the 2006 National Survey on Drug Use and Health showed that for people aged between twelve and 20 about 30 per cent (10.8 million) admitted drinking alcohol in the previous month, and approximately 19 per cent (7.2 million) were binge drinkers.

Alcohol Focus Scotland, alcohol's equivalent of Action and Smoking and Health (ASH), said there was substantial evidence that increasing the cost of alcohol could reduce alcohol abuse. It therefore supports minimum pricing for alcohol. The evidence staring any visitor to continental Europe in the face is that cheap booze has no such anti-social effect. In fact the effect of putting the cost of alcohol up to reduce 'binge drinking' has to be questioned. As Freya Walkley argued on *The Free Society* website, "Put the price of vodka up!! People can afford an extra 55p. It makes no difference to a group of people who are going threes on a bottle."[7]

The problem, as we have already seen with tobacco taxation, is that the higher the price relative to the real cost of production or the price in other countries leads to an explosion in counterfeiting and smuggling. Governments do not need to go down this bullying, coercive route, making criminals out of otherwise law-abiding people. The evidence is there for all to see that if our constabulary returned to more traditional methods of law enforcement there would be no need for restrictions on law abiding, moderate drinkers who form the vast majority of consumers.

Recently in Ayrshire a return by police to what I describe as 'more traditional methods' – what the public would call bobbies on the beat – saw a reduction in anti-social behaviour and alcohol fuelled crimes by more than half, and in one area as much as 66 per cent. Extra officers were drafted in for high-visibility patrols, targeting crime hot spots and using stop and search when there was suspicious behaviour. Commenting on their methods, police superintendent John Haslett, sub-divisional officer in Ayr, said: "Local intelligence would suggest it is a small minority of people that is responsible for this intimidating behaviour. We will continue to patrol Castlehill Woods and Roselle Park on foot and on bicycles to tackle the issues of youths hanging around, drinking and causing disruption."

A pilot scheme to ban off licence sales of alcohol to people under 21 in towns such as Armadale in West Lothian, and Cupar in Fife is said to have reduced vandalism by up to 60 per cent. No doubt the trial was accompanied by greater enforcement with the police adopting a higher visibility. The message seems clear. Alcohol-fuelled crime can be reduced by putting more constables on visible pro-active policing, leaving ordinary citizens to get on with their lives without restricting their liberties any further. All that is required is for the police to do their job effectively, a task made easier if politicians don't saddle them with all sorts of responsibilities to engage with communities. The best way to build community links to prevent crime is by effectively catching those that commit it. In Glasgow there was a 38 per cent reduction in serious assaults after city centre zones were flooded by police foot patrols at weekends and nights. Earlier in the year in Edinburgh the reintroduction of foot patrols by bobbies with local knowledge of the area and its people had reduced crime substantially. The method had not been used since the early 1990s.

The public wants action but not the action that the politicians are offering. Out of 13 measures offered by pollsters in a survey carried out after the SNP published its proposals, the overwhelming majority of Scots said they wanted to see tougher action by the authorities on off-licences that sell to underage drinkers, better education in schools, and more regular arrests of drunks. "Irresponsible parents", "peer pressure" and "Scotland's historic drinking culture" were among the main reasons cited by Scots for underage drinking. "Taxes on drink being too low" was well down the list. It was ranked ninth by the public, hardly a great endorsement to increase taxation to counteract underage drinking.[8]

In a separate piece of research the Scottish Social Attitudes Survey found that less than half of those asked could state the recommended daily alcohol unit intake for men and women, despite a long list of expensive public education campaigns. Roughly half knew that the number of alcohol units in a single measure of spirits or a pint of beer but only 15 per cent knew that a bottle of wine contained between eight and ten units. Women's physical limitations were better understood with 41 per cent identifying that the advisable daily limit for women was two to three units, but only 34 per cent knew that men are recommended to drink no more than three to four units a day.

The failure to communicate its message about the recommended levels of alcohol consumption explains why the state has moved from nanny to bully mode. The truth is that the practice of drinking alcohol across the week on a daily basis is related to lifestyle, age and disposable income and is probably not the norm for the British public and even less so in the United States where alcohol consumption is less and often frowned upon. Instead people still look towards the weekend as their main time for the consumption of intoxicating liquor and if the units consumed in an evening were to be measured many otherwise fine upstanding pillars of society would discover that they too fell into the category of being a 'binge drinker'.

Alcohol Concern claims that 40 per cent of all male drinking sessions are binge-drinking sessions; likewise 22 per cent of female drinking sessions; and binge-drinking has risen significantly over the last three years. Does this surprise anyone when the relaxed social drinking of the past has, for a variety of reasons, been squeezed into smaller slots of our weekly lifestyles? A glass of wine or a pint at lunchtime? Oh no, you don't. A couple of drinks after work to unwind before catching the train or the bus home? Oh no, you don't. Get down to the gym!

When I worked in London in the Eighties a half pint or a pint at lunch was normal. So was a couple of pints after work once or twice a week. Not enough to make it a binge but a recorded incident of drinking nonetheless. Then on a Friday or a Saturday (but rarely both because of the cost) I would have maybe four pints, perhaps even a few drams. Today this would probably be called binge-drinking even though it would be spread over three or four hours and might involve some food. So maybe one out of six instances of my drinking could be reported as 'binging'. Today new pressures, including the nannying and bullying by my public sector employers, have reduced my social drinking so I don't drink any alcohol at lunchtime at all and I only have one drink after work and one night out at the weekend. Suddenly my Saturday night out, which has not changed in any way, is responsible for half my alcohol intake and I am 'binging' in 50 per cent of my drinking sessions compared to only 16.6 per cent before, an escalation that makes for a good headline and can be used to justify more pressures to control my drinking. And yet my overall consumption of alcohol has fallen!!

We're told that alcohol consumption is a cause of considerable national expense. Hospital admissions directly linked to excess alcohol have more than doubled in the past ten years; alcohol-related crimes and accidents have risen sharply; it causes domestic violence, traffic accidents and other social ills. There has of course been a change in social drinking habits and not all of it has been to my liking but a great deal of the rise in statistics is the degree to which women now drink alcohol throughout the week. In the 'bad' old days women had their drinks bought for them by men. If they were alone they would often drink in the snug, not in the men's bar or even the lounge. Now women populate the bars and lounges. They order rounds, they buy men drink, they are in nearly every respect equal and so they are appearing in alcohol-related statistics that were once the preserve of men.

We're also told that "5.9 million people drink more than twice the recommended daily guidelines on some occasions". On some occasions? Is that really a terrible anti-social thing to do? You can see where this is going. 'Passive drinking' and its effects will become the next big lifestyle crusade. What effects, you may ask? "The 'passive effects' of alcohol misuse are catastrophic – rape, sexual assault, domestic and other violence, drunk driving and street disorder – alcohol affects thousands more innocent victims than passive smoking." So says a leaflet on the Alcohol Health Alliance's website. This means we shall have a new group of people 'at risk', the 'passive drinkers' who will need to be protected from the ordinary drinkers.

This apocalyptic turn of events is already bubbling to the surface. In 2008 Edinburgh City Council gave serious consideration to limiting the number of people who would be allowed to stand in a pub, not because of any concern for personal safety from crushing or a fire risk, but to try and discourage people from buying a round of drinks. What business is it of the council's, one may ask? After much ridicule in the local media the Labour politicians backed down, but the initiative had all the usual 'experts' saying it was a good idea and providing junk evidence as justification for the councillors' position.

Standing or sitting, it's not that difficult to exceed the guidelines of four units for a male and three units for a female and suddenly you've become a 'binge-drinker'. Indeed, if it makes anyone feel better, let me admit to enjoying my fourth glass of wine while reviewing and rewriting this chapter on a Lufthansa flight home from Nigeria. Another glass and I'll be a binge-drinker, at 40,000 feet! I'm perfectly rational, I can type and I shall smile at the passport official when we land. I know I'm not fit to drive or operate a lathe but I have no intention of doing either. I simply want to enjoy some fine French wine on a very long journey home.

It is this clash between people's own understanding or experience and the hectoring hegemony of public health bullies, lumping everyone together and treating us all like children or, worse, law breakers, instead of targeting those responsible for breaking the law, that frustrates people. It was this attitude that brought us the unnecessary ban on alcohol on London Transport by the new mayor of London Boris Johnson. Instead of doing the hard job, policing the Tube more effectively against genuine lager louts, Johnson took the easy option and penalised everyone. Arguments about whether or not the ban was a good thing miss the point. The ban on alcohol is simply an admission that the Tube cannot be policed effectively.

I am not arguing that nothing should be done by politicians and governments to stop anti-social drunken behaviour, but they must start by treating the overwhelming majority like the sensible, mature adults we are. They must explain the hard challenges that we face, in choices, consequences and costs, and then focus on the miscreants who abuse our freedoms and put them at risk for those who respect them and take the responsibility that goes with them. We can have relatively cheap alcohol, we can have liberal licensing hours, and we can be left to make our own judgements about how much we should drink, when we should drink and where we should drink, but when we encroach on other peoples' liberties by over-indulgence, a lack of good judgement or pure evil-mindedness, then we should expect the law to take its course, not shrink behind high taxation, petty restrictions and a shaming denormalisation that tars us all with the same brush.

Notes:

1. *Daily Telegraph*, 6 September 2009
2. *Scottish Daily Mail*, 17 July 2008
3. The logical conclusion of "It's society's fault" is that it is everybody's fault, including the victims, except for those who committed the offence. Margaret Thatcher famously challenged the unwillingness of people to accept responsibility when she said in an interview (*Woman's Own*, 31 October 1987), "There is no such thing as society. There is living tapestry of men and women and people and the beauty of that tapestry and the quality of our lives will depend upon how much each of us is prepared to take responsibility for ourselves and each of us prepared to turn round and help by our own efforts those who are unfortunate."
4. *Daily Telegraph*, 3 September 2008
5. *Scottish Daily Express*, 8 October 2008
6. *The Scotsman*, 6 September 2008
7. Freya Walkley, *Some of us just want to have fun*, The Free Society, 14 March 2008
8. 1,000 Scots polled by ICM for the Wine and Spirits Trade Association (WSTA) and reported in the *Scotland on Sunday* 2008.

# Chapter Seven

# BIG BULLY IS WATCHING YOU

*"Relying on the government to protect your privacy
is like asking a peeping tom to install your window blinds."*

- JOHN PERRY BARLOW

George Orwell, Aldous Huxley, Freidrich Hayek and Patrick McGoohan were right.

It was George Orwell who in 1948 wrote of a world where the authorities knew your every move, where you are free to do what you wish as long as it conforms to the role you have been given in the state's centrally planned lifestyle straitjacket. He turned the numbers of the year round and famously called the book *Nineteen Eighty-four*.[1]

It was Aldous Huxley who told us how in the new scientific age we shouldn't fear the cataclysmic end it threatens but rather the slow and inexorable stupefaction of the individual and the ability to defend our liberties and ourselves as we are conditioned to consume only those bountiful pleasures the state approves of. In his aptly titled *Brave New World* he warned how our world would end, to paraphrase T S Eliot's verse, not with a bang, but a simper.[2]

It was Friedrich Hayek who in his seminal work warned us that we should fear less the dictator who so obviously can be seen for what he is and can be challenged. Instead it is the social democrat who, in employing centralised planning of the state to right all our economic and social ills, incrementally removes our freedoms until we become tools of their great plan for society. He called his book *The Road To Serfdom* and despite a few reverses it is the road we have been travelling down for much of the last 60 years.[3]

And it was Patrick McGoohan who brought many of these arguments to life in his ground-breaking television series *The Prisoner*. Ostensibly about a former secret agent who mysteriously resigns, it raises far larger questions about the relationship between the individual and society and just how much of our lives we do control and how much is shaped for us.[4]

These works have much in common. They all explained how the actions of those in power would be justified by demanding individual sacrifice towards the greater good of society. Group rights would transcend individual rights and if you didn't give up your individual freedoms they would be taken away from you. Forget the uncomfortable facts that history repeatedly tells us; that man is fallible, regularly makes mistakes and can be unbelievably cruel and violent to his neighbour, even his own family. Just give him a cause to believe in and the absolute power that corrupts absolutely will be used, with the seductive justification that it is for the greater good, to force us to behave according to the great plan. People who accept that the state should act in this way are essentially saying that we are born as slaves to society and then granted freedoms when the state, its political elite or a faceless bureaucrat, decides it is in their interests to do so.

They have it the wrong way around. We are born free and we consent to some of those freedoms being sacrificed so that the rule of law and compassionate welfare systems can make an often harsh and unfair world more just, more palatable, and even enjoyable. The police can (and I believe should) be given greater resources so that we have more bobbies on our streets than there are traffic wardens. We should expand the courts to deal with violent crime and, if we must, we can even build another prison or two to detain those who have taken our property or used violence against us (assuming that we accept that prison works, which is an altogether different debate). We can do all these things and probably more without invading our privacy or reducing our rights.

We should not give up our liberties lightly, however. As a member of the Scottish Parliament I once undertook a surgery tour of rural Perthshire and was taken aback when an agitated constituent confronted me in Callander. He didn't have a problem with care for the elderly (or the lack of it) or the local council road repairs (or the lack of them). His complaint was different and, I thought, rather bizarre. When he arrived from Switzerland, the country of his birth, to settle in Scotland he reported to the police so they knew of his arrival and his whereabouts. The police, he told me, were indifferent. They said he wasn't required to do this and that it was of no consequence to them. He then reported directly to Stirling Council so that they also knew of his arrival and his whereabouts. They too appeared indifferent and said that they would change their records in order to collect council tax but as they amend their records annually his presence would have come to their attention anyway. Although it happened many years ago it still rankled enough for my Swiss constituent to ask how can we run a country efficiently without the authorities knowing where we are and what we are all doing. I replied that we do things differently in Britain and I wouldn't like to see our customs change.

That was before September 11th, 2001. Suddenly there were calls for the introduction of identity cards in the fight against terrorism with the same old proposals that surface every time there is a law enforcement problem. Football hooligans? Give them identity cards. Under-age drinkers? Give them identity cards. Asylum seekers? Give them identity cards. The mantra is the same each time. The state, it seems, cannot solve our social ills without knowing who we are and where we are.

I accept that the atrocities in New York and Washington, and those in Bali, Madrid and London, were far more serious than a passing social problem. There was a new war against terrorism (not to be mistaken with the later war against Iraq) and in times of war even a free democratic country may require methods that would normally be rejected in times of peace. We had identity cards in the Second World War and there might be a case for them again for a limited period, but when I considered the arguments used in the wake of 9/11 I concluded that we were being duped.

For me the only case that merits the introduction of ID cards is if they were to make a significant contribution to the prevention or discovery of more terrorist acts in Britain. For ID cards to work they have to be compulsory. That means it must become a criminal offence not to carry an ID card on your person. Turning up within a week at a police station to show your papers, as you do for a road traffic accident, would defeat the purpose. If they are compulsory then every resident must be entitled to have one. This means that all current or future supporters of Osama Bin Laden and Al Qaeda who already live in Britain will have identity cards. It also means that all economic migrants and foreign students will be entitled to them quite legitimately, whether they are potential terrorists or not.

If I can think up a number of schemes to obtain a false ID card then so will terrorists. And then there are the racketeers who will open up a new black market as they find ways to obtain illicit or counterfeit cards. Using technology to make them foolproof only makes them more expensive to introduce without preventing the illegal trade. Indeed it will drive the black market value up and create a perverse incentive for organised criminals to invest in the necessary equipment to overcome the technical obstacles.

What affect did ID cards have in Germany where so many of the terrorists are thought to have operated initially? None, because the foreign nationals were all there legitimately. ID cards cannot and will not prevent 'sleepers' from travelling. Does anyone really believe that if Britain had used ID cards in Ulster the IRA would not have overcome this hurdle fairly quickly?

When he introduced the idea the then home secretary David Blunkett anticipated additional roles for ID cards in our womb to tomb welfare state. It wouldn't just be the police who could ask to see our cards. That right would be extended to every official of every rank, and once it becomes the norm the danger is that ID cards will remain with us forever.

In 1950, five years after the end of the Second World War, people were still required to have an identity card. They might be with us still if it wasn't for Clarence Henry Willcock. We owe him a great deal. While there was no suggestion that Willcock had been driving erratically, PC Harold Muckle ordered Willcock to pull over and asked him to produce his national registration card, the ID card of its time. Willcock refused and failed to turn up at the local police station with his identity document two days later. He was charged under the provisions of the 1939 National Registration Act that had been introduced because of the national emergency of war. Willcock fought his case on the basis that as the national emergency of war had passed it was wrong for the police to continue to use the powers granted to them, powers that had, after all, been intended as temporary. The local magistrates, whilst finding him guilty (they could do nothing else), gave him an absolute discharge. The Crown appealed and Willcock's case went all the way to the High Court where seven judges not only upheld but also commended the magistrates on their decision.

The 1951 court case attracted enormous publicity and Willcock received a great deal of public sympathy for his principled stand. In October 1951 Winston Churchill's Conservative government was elected to power on the slogan 'Set the People Free' and subsequently abolished both identity cards and food rationing. The likes of Clarence Willcock, who went back to the anonymity of his dry-cleaning shop, are the people who make the biggest difference to our lives. People who believe in something and are willing, without violence, without threats and without bullying to argue their case and risk losing a great deal for the rights of others.

With the state intervening so much in our lives today does anyone really believe we could rid ourselves of ID cards if and when we conquer terrorism? This time it is not just a dog-eared piece of card with a photo and some basic details. In the twenty-first century time an ID card has the ability to contain all our personal details as well as our fingerprints and an iris scan.

Various governments have proposed the introduction of identity cards, including the Conservatives when Michael Howard was home secretary. In 2002 Labour home secretary David Blunkett told the House of Commons that the ID card would reduce benefit fraud and help combat illegal immigration. People had nothing to fear, he said. He wasn't proposing to grant police the power to produce the card on demand. That's all very well, but what happens when governments change? What value would the word of a former home secretary hold then? Since that speech we have had four home secretaries and a new prime minister. It only takes one minister with a different view and a change in government policy can happen overnight.

The ability of modern technology to hold all types of information from different sources, including health records, finances, employment records on a single card is truly frightening. Supporters of ID cards say it will counter fraud, ignoring the scale of credit card and bank card fraud that modern technology has made possible. Does it not concern home secretaries that by stealing, copying and manufacturing ID cards fraudsters will have access to far more information than they can currently get their hands on?

The Home Office has always argued that faked chips would be spotted at border checkpoints because they would not match key codes when checked against an international database. What international database? Following the 9/11 attacks, when many of the bombers had travelled using fake passports, the USA demanded that other countries adopt biometric passports. Forty-five countries have since issued over 100 million microchipped passports in the belief that they will defeat terrorists and make international travel safer, with Britain introducing e-passports in March 2006. The passports contain a tiny radio frequency chip and antenna attached to the inside back page. A special electronic reader operated by the customs official issues an encrypted signal and the chip responds by sending back the holder's ID and biometric details. But only ten of the 45 countries with e-passports have signed up to the public key directory code system, and only five are using it. Britain is a member and is due to start using the directory this year but the system will be secure only if every e-passport country has joined.

And what do we mean by 'secure'? An expose by *The Times* in 2008 suggests that microchips are vulnerable to cloning and bogus biometrics can be inserted in fake or blank passports. In fact the paper blew apart the British government's claim that microchip passports are the security solution of the future. Foolproof against identity theft? The paper showed how they could be cloned in a matter of minutes and accepted as genuine by the computer software now in use at Manchester Airport.[5]

The tests for *The Times* were conducted by Jeroen van Beek, a security researcher at the University of Amsterdam. Using his own software, a publicly available programing code, a £40 card reader and two £10 RFID chips, van Beek took less than an hour to clone and manipulate two passport chips to a level at which they were ready to be planted inside fake or stolen passports so they can be accepted as genuine by Golden Reader, the standard software used by the International Civil Aviation Organisation and recommended for use at airports. A baby boy's passport chip was altered to contain an image of Osama bin Laden, and the passport of a 36-year-old woman was changed to feature a picture of Hiba Darghmeh, a Palestinian suicide bomber who killed three people in 2003. They worked.

This embarrassment also undermined claims that the 3,000 blank passports stolen before use were worthless because they couldn't be forged. Well, that is clearly up for challenge now. The ability to clone chips leaves travellers open to identity theft when they surrender their passports to hotels or car rental companies. Criminals in countries open to bribery, fraud and corruption could pay or blackmail back office staff to read the chips and clone them. The original passport holder's name and date of birth could be left on the fake chip, but with the picture, fingerprints and other biometric data of a criminal client added. The stolen identity could then be used by a criminal or terrorist to travel the world with the original passport holder being none the wiser.

The Government's £4 billion identity card scheme relies on the same biometric technology and is expected to contain similar microchips carrying up to 50 pieces of personal and biometric information about their holders. How long before someone, or a newspaper like *The Times*, demonstrates that the ID cards can be cloned and false ones made up just like these passports?

For those not worried about the technological failures of passports or ID cards the standard refrain from law-abiding people is to say "Why worry if you are innocent?" Well, let me ask, have you ever had trouble at a cash machine, a supermarket till or a department store with your bank, credit or store card, and it wasn't your fault? Was it not embarrassing, humiliating and annoying? Have you ever found that records kept on you or your family are wildly incorrect or out of date? As a former MSP who dealt with constituents' problems, and being a member of the card carrying human race, I know these problems not only exist but are commonplace. Do we honestly wish the authorities to have powers that can damage our lives or, worse still, allow that information to fall into the hands of criminals? Can you imagine the difficulties that might arise if your identity card let you down and you could no longer prove who you are?

Then there is the ability of the British government to repeatedly lose, in one way or another, the information it holds, which in the case of an ID card could mean everything about you. Take, for instance, the names, addresses and bank details of people who receive child benefit. Child benefit is a universal benefit paid to everyone with children, including the prime minister's wife and some of the wealthiest people in the country. To organised criminals, these bank accounts are not just handy, they could be valuable beyond their wildest dreams. So for the UK to lose a complete set of child benefit records was no minor misfortune. And the government knew it, because it recognised that a link would be made to the potential for losing identity card information too. And so it was that the most brazen statements by ministers were saved for defending the government's commitment to the identity card. It's no use saying there will be extra security checks for identity card information so it won't be lost. The fact is that simpler systems have been ignored and a more complicated method must be open to even more errors.

I am not alone in seeing the potential for trouble that ID cards and existing technologies present. Edward Garnier QC, Conservative MP for Harborough, said in a standing committee debate: "The [Identity Cards] Bill is designed to print across our foreheads a human barcode. Those who do not wish to understand the seriousness of what the Bill represents in terms of the change in the culture and society in which we live are failing in their duties as representatives of the public."[6]

For me the civil liberties issues are enough to oppose ID cards, but many more are just as concerned by the practicalities of administering such a system. Currently, 15 million national insurance numbers cannot be accounted for while the British Cattle Movement Service lost 93,000 identities in 2003 alone, despite having the latest computerised systems. Now that's cattle and they don't commit fraud. Human error was completely responsible.

The state does not just make human errors with the management of all the information it holds about us. It also plays fast and loose with it. Thanks to rigorous parliamentary questioning by Liberal Democrat MP Jenny Willott who also gathered information using the Freedom of Information Act, it has come to light that on five occasions since 2004 private firms with police contracts have successfully applied to use the UK's DNA database to help them develop computer programs.[7]

The database contains records of 4.2 million people of whom a million have never been convicted of an offence. Records are rarely deleted, even when a person is not charged. It is not just civil rights groups and freedom lovers across Britain that are critical of the DNA database. A highly critical report from the government's genetics watchdog has called for the database to have more management safeguards.

While ministers repeatedly say that the database is vital to solving crimes there was never so much as a hint that private businesses would have access to profiles for commercial purposes. Thankfully the companies involved were not given the identities of the people whose DNA profiles they analysed, but like the loss of all sorts of digitalised information it's not beyond the bounds of possibility that a mistake will be made and the identities are not removed or the wrong file is passed on, or a less than scrupulous person could seek to sell on additional information. These scenarios are all 'what ifs' and it is always possible to be sanguine and think, don't worry, that wouldn't happen, but the wave of errors that has come to light in the last year with Revenue and Customs, the Ministry of Defence, the intelligence services and Health and Social Security all managing to lose, misplace, wrongly address or leave information on trains suggests that it is only a matter of time before the same happens to information held on the DNA database.

The advance of technology takes the old national registration card into new territory because it won't be a stand alone ID card but, after the passage of time, it will almost certainly be linked to the national DNA database and if the authorities have their way that database will eventually include everyone, irrespective of whether we have ever committed a crime or not. Already there are platoons of police and politicians trying to justify the inclusion of people absolved of any crime (in England and Wales but not Scotland where the law requires such records to be destroyed) despite the

European courts ruling it as a breach of human rights. Some have suggested that in future everyone should be added to the database at birth.

An example of what can happen when the zealousness of authorities is combined with an unwillingness to admit error and the loss of all sense of proportion and balance comes in this little story from Welwyn Garden City in January of 2008. Fourteen–year-old Alex Digby bought a 50p copy of a daily newspaper on his way to school at Martin's newsagent on Woodhall Parade. (Boy buys newspaper to read. Sounds commendable to me.) Anyway, he was sitting outside a petrol station on Stanborough Road when he was accused of stealing the paper from the forecourt shop, arrested by an off-duty policeman, taken to a police station and locked up alone in a cell where was kept for four hours until his name was cleared.[8]

His parents were understandably non-plussed by the authorities' handling of the theft allegation that has left Alex's DNA and photograph on a national register for life even though their son is not guilty. His mum said: "It could have been handled in a completely different way. He only bought the paper because he wanted to see the football odds for Arsenal, but no-one would listen to him." His father added: "He has never been in trouble with the police. Why should he be on there? "

The *Welwyn & Hatfield Times* reported: "A police spokeswoman said chief constable Frank Whiteley had the power to remove people from the database, but Alex Digby's profile would remain on file. No reason was given as to why." So what did the police think they were doing taking the boy's DNA, fingerprints and photograph while they worked out what had happened over the possible theft of a 50p newspaper? What justification does the chief constable have for retaining this personal information and why won't he release it?

I can recall in my youth that some of my mates used to think it was great fun to climb garden walls and 'raid' a ripe apple tree. I never found this a remotely attractive pursuit, but some thought it was a great laugh, even though many of them had apple trees in their own back gardens! Occasionally they would get nabbed by the local police. If caught they would be given a strict dressing down and taken back to their homes to be reprimanded all over again. It was all about the thrill of danger, of being chased and not getting caught. It was never about the usually sour crab apples. Today they are all adults and none of them have been convicted of any crime. Indeed some of them went on to work for the police and the fire service.

After reading about Alex Digby's experience I wondered where Britain is heading and how we should treat kids who get up to no good occasionally but are not remotely of a criminal disposition. Is the approach now to simply put everyone together and collect their DNA, fingerprints and photographs so in future they can be swept for a match? If that is the case then we are a small step from having our DNA taken at birth so we can be monitored for the rest of our lives. In fact, with DNA now so important in bringing criminals to justice, some people are calling for a national DNA database that would keep on file the records of 60 million individuals living in Britain.

Calling for a universal database, Stephen House, chief constable of Strathclyde Police, said that storing the genetic profiles of every man, woman and child would be of benefit because it would help catch more criminals. He said: "Forget criminality, we'll take DNA from everyone in the country. If the public and the government decide they want to do it, you would do it gradually. One of the ways to do it is that you would say all newborn children would have DNA recorded and when you apply for a driver's licence your DNA would be taken and gradually over the years would start to develop a 100 per cent database. Would it deter people? That's less certain, but we would detect more crime."[9]

Lord Justice Sedley, one of England's most experienced appeal court judges, has also called for a national database. He described the country's current system as "indefensible" and said: "We have a situation where if you happen to have been in the hands of the police, then your DNA is on permanent record. If you haven't, it isn't ... that's broadly the picture. It also means that a great many people who are walking the streets, and whose DNA would show them guilty of crimes, go free." [10]

In 2008 Stephen Wright was convicted of murdering five women in Ipswich the previous year. It is thought he may also have been responsible for others going back as far as the early Nineties. In the same week of that conviction Levi Bellfield was found guilty of two murders and an attempted murder and is now under investigation for 20 other similar attacks, including the murder of schoolgirl Milly Dowling. DNA played a significant part in those convictions.

So why not help the police in this way? The issue comes back to the presumption of innocence. We are all innocent until, beyond reasonable doubt, we are proven guilty. It's this presumption of innocence that has previously deterred Britain from having a national database of fingerprints. After the revelations of abuse of fingerprint evidence in Scotland, would you trust the authorities with your prints or your DNA? Computers made the massive task of a national fingerprint register possible a long time ago but it is the unacceptable infringement of our liberties that stops politicians from taking such an invasive step. Of course having DNA records can help the police, and I support the retention of the DNA of convicted criminals, but the day we make it compulsory for everyone is the day we give up our presumption of innocence. On that day we all become guilty.

What most members of the public are unaware of is how the advances in DNA sweeping are actually making the use of DNA for prosecution more problematic, rather than easier. A detective who has used DNA evidence told me the process is now so sensitive that it is working against itself. To take samples of DNA at the scene of a crime now requires such so many measures to eliminate cross-contamination that a great deal of the so-called evidence is immediately dismissed if the correct procedures, which may be impractical in the circumstances, are not followed. Then there is the problem of confirming that the DNA of suspects was actually left at the scene of the crime at the time the crime was committed. The fact that even the slightest DNA, compared to what had to be gathered in the past, can place people at a crime scene could lead to innocent people facing prosecution and long-term jail sentences. Those who support DNA registers in the name of pragmatism, believing that it is worth the loss of at least one civil liberty because it delivers results, may find that their belief evaporates as the science and technology improves even more and suddenly they too become a potential suspect!

The surveillance society extends beyond ID cards and a universal DNA database and into the satellite technology of GPRS and the use of CCTV. Saudi Arabia is to trial a new dashboard mounted satellite-based display system that shows the speed limit of the road you are driving on and the speed you are travelling. If you break the limit you are given a warning to reduce your speed. If you consistently ignore this warning the word 'Ticket' then flashes up and a speeding ticket is sent to your home address.

Very good, you might say, just imagine how that will make all the drivers in the UK obey the speed limits. Perhaps. Then again, given that so many people drive without insurance or even a licence, we can once again expect the majority of reasonable drivers to be clobbered while the genuinely dangerous offenders will remain untraceable. What is disturbing to me is that this is another example of how the state, using (or abusing) new technology can control our lives. Worse, the state will be in possession of even more information about our whereabouts. Put this little device, which at any given time knows what street we're on (or what street our car is on), into an ID card and there is very little that the state won't know about you. No doubt it will include your DNA profile too.

The temptation to exploit the policing and security 'advantages' by combining different technologies like GPRS and ID card chips will become irresistible to politicians. Slowly, and insidiously, this technology will dominate our lives. At the moment politicians who support ID cards say they will only be compulsory when we apply for a new passport. It's a short leap from there to making ID cards compulsory (and we will be charged £300 for the privilege). Then, following another terrorist outrage, perhaps, it will become compulsory to carry your ID card on you at all times. In the meantime shops, banks, restaurants and all sorts of places will ask to swipe your identity card to verify who you are before recording your financial transaction.

In due course, at the click of a few keys, officials will be able to pull together your national insurance number, your taxes due and paid, your religion, race, state of health, bank balance, credit rating, the cafe where you bought your coffee and croissant at 8.39am, where you bought your subscription to *Amateur Photographer* and, thanks to this new dashboard devil, where you are at 9.17am. Put this technology on an ID card and within ten years the state will know everything there is to know about you and where you are at any given moment.

It may sound fanciful and alarmist but there would be little difficulty placing a microchip in the back of our hand, for example. (If we can put microchips in pets we can put them in humans.) When shopping at Waitrose or the Co-op the teller will simply scan the back of your hand like a barcode to deduct your money and relay to the faceless ones what you have bought, where and when. All of this will happen slowly and incrementally so that resistance is low. But it could happen unless we nip it in the bud now before new surveillance society develops momentum.

Just as campaigners continue to demand the extension of the smoking ban to outdoor parks and beaches, with exclusion zones around public buildings, so the goals of those who advocate a genuine surveillance society know no limits. (As with tobacco, food and drink it's all being done in "our best interests".) Not content with monitoring where we go, at what speed we travel, and so on, we are routinely watch by CCTV cameras in every high street and shopping mall in the country. More sinister, is it possible that our children and grandchildren may be monitored from birth in order to steer them away from becoming criminals.

An alarming story appeared in the *Daily Telegraph* in April 2008 when the paper's home affairs editor Philip Johnson revealed that: "A Downing Street review of law and order also foreshadowed greater use of sophisticated CCTV, an expanded DNA database and 'instant justice' powers for police." Apparently, since ministers believe that most crime is committed by a small number of offenders, who can be identified at birth, the focus should change away from the 'offence' towards the 'offender'.[11] The idea is to use 'triggers' such as when a child's parent goes to jail or is known for taking illegal drugs. This is an extension of current practice whereby social welfare and children's services departments already monitor a set number of children who have become known to them through truancy or other recorded problems, and it will be supported by a database for all English and Welsh children available in 2009. The database will include the child and parents' names and include a "facility for practitioners to indicate to others that they have information to share, are taking action, or have undertaken an assessment, in relation to a child".

The move to create such a database (without DNA records but that's only a matter of time) came about as a response to the tragic death of Victoria Climbie in the belief that it could prevent a repeat of the failures that contributed to her being neglected by both parents and the social services. Once identified the children will be subject to measures such as home visits from specialists. If the government believes that certain 'traits' such as having a short attention span or living in a deprived environment will lead to a life of crime then how is it intending to respond – by removing children from their families because they are poor?

The state is not prepared to allow parents to fail in their responsibilities and is aiming to become a supra-national parent taking on all responsibility for future generations. Of course when the state fails to detect some aspect of poor child-rearing that ultimately results in the death of a youngster such as Victoria Climbie, then rather than admit that its human or technical systems failed and consider if it should reorganise its service delivery, reinvest more heavily in capable personnel (or both), it calls for greater intervention and the gathering of even more information through extended surveillance.

Irrespective of the civil liberties issues, the sheer scale of the task suggests that the enormous financial costs involved will be in vain as it is bound to end in more tragic failure. I can almost hear the coroner's report being read out now: a failure to monitor the information, a failure to co-ordinate the different services, a failure to communicate between services, a failure to keep appointments, a failure to notice various signs at a child's home and record them, a failure of a school to record truancy accurately thus not triggering an intervention etc etc.

The state will ask to be given more controls, more powers of entry, more, more, more. And children will still die. Indeed it was only after I first drafted this chapter that the death of 'Baby P' became a national scandal in December 2008. 'Baby P' will not be the last victim of cruelty to children. Perhaps if the existing services just did their job properly and used existing laws more children would be saved from evil or neglectful parents? The sad irony is that if there is a marker or a trigger that suggests that someone is heading from an early age to a lifetime of crime, the child will no doubt be taken into care by the state. The premise that the state can do a better job than parents, when all the available evidence shows that children in care have worse lifetime prospects, is turning the truth on its head. The point of any state intervention should be to make it brief and to involve family-based solutions such as foster parents and adoption. (Ironically, some councils are choosing to ban adults who smoke from fostering young children, thus reducing the number of foster carers in the system.)

To change the mentality that the state knows best and has an undisputed right to intervene, we have to reassert the idea that individuals should be left alone to live their lives as they see fit and it is only when we infringe seriously upon the rights of others that the state has a legitimate reason to intervene. When a child's health or welfare is seriously at risk the state has a duty to seek the protection of that child through the courts, but we have to draw a line otherwise the triggers for state intervention could easily include such fashionable bête-noirs as parents who smoke or drink or are 'obese'.

Notes:

1. George Orwell, *1984*, Continuum, London, 1948
2. Aldous Huxley, *Brave New World*, Continuum, Chatto & Windus, 1932
3. Friederich von Hayek, *Road to Serfdom*, Continuum, London, 1945
4. Patrick McGoohan, *The Prisoner*, ITC, London, 1967
5. *The Times*, 6 August 2008, 'Fakeproof' e-passport is cloned in minutes
6. Edward Garnier QC, Conservative MP for Harborough
7. *Daily Telegraph*, 25 July 2008
8. *Welwyn & Hatfield Times*
9. Auslan Cramb, *Daily Telegraph*, 6 August 2008
   There are around 4.2 million DNA profiles stored in England, the largest genetic database in the world while, in Scotland the database holds around 200,000.
10. *Guardian*, 5 September 2007
11. Philip Johnson, *Daily Telegraph*, 19 April 2008

# Chapter Eight

# THE HUNGER FOR MORE CONTROL

*"The smallest minority on earth is the individual.*
*Those who deny individual rights, cannot claim*
*to be defenders of minorities."*

- AYN RAND

The latest regulations on smoking or alcohol or trans fats are justified by the authorities because they 'send a positive message' about what is acceptable or unacceptable. In place of public information films advising people how to improve their lives, modern government increasingly uses the law to force people to do this or do that. You hear politicians talking about evidence-based policies but usually its lip service. They are far more interested in enforcing their own ideology and prejudices rather than establishing a basis of evidence. Nanny, who has developed into a fully-fledged bully, has an insatiable hunger for more and more petty rules and regulations.

People were still coming to terms with the smoking ban in England when the idea of making smokers get a permit to buy tobacco was raised in October 2007 by Professor Julian Le Grand, chairman of Health England and Tony Blair's former senior health advisor. Flying a kite? Possibly, but it's all part of the softening-up process. Ideas are floated in the media and if only a small number of people object or make a fuss there's a real danger that it will be advocated more seriously and then introduced, often in a very short space of time.

What is a permit but a licence granted by an authority to either maintain a certain standard of performance or quality of supply or to control numbers, such as limiting the number of anglers to preserve a river's stock of fish. So what would a licence to smoke mean? Would it mean that an applicant would have to meet a certain standard of health to qualify for a permit? What would happen if, having acquired a permit, you fell below those standards? Would the permit be withdrawn? Meanwhile I can already see a British Medical Association press statement being drafted in readiness to extend the permit's power: "BMA says pregnant women should have smoking permits withdrawn" or "BMA says poor health in Glasgow could be reduced by withdrawing more smoking permits".

According to Le Grand, there is nothing illiberal about a smoking permit. People, he says, will still be able to smoke. True, but it's another step towards the denormalisation of smokers that anti-smoking campaigners hope will lead, eventually, to the complete prohibition of smoking. Like taxation the cost of the permit will be increased annually. By raising the price and tightening the qualifications fewer and fewer people will apply for a permit. This will breed resentment because smoking will be portrayed as a rich man's habit. Eventually, in order to create a level playing field, smoking tobacco will be declared illegal. Fanciful? I don't think so.

As with all modern day tobacco controls, the nanny state has been replaced by the bully state. The idea is to make smokers feel like lepers, social pariahs. The hope is that the non-smoking majority will turn against them. But the bully state is not just gunning for smokers. After smokers it will be drinkers, drivers, those who are overweight – anybody, in fact, the lifestyle fascists wish to control. The 'licence to smoke' will become a special licence to drink alcohol, eat fatty foods, drive a 4x4 and all manner of things we currently take for granted.

Meanwhile the hunger for more control goes on, pushing and prodding to find where smokers might concede some more ground. The lessons learned are then applied to fight against obesity or salt levels or alcohol consumption. Removing the display of tobacco in shops, forcing them to be kept out of sight, is "the next logical step" in the war on tobacco. Writing on The Free Society website, Eamonn Butler, director of the Adam Smith Institute, commented: "I don't smoke and don't care much for smoking, but haven't we persecuted smokers enough? I wonder which other of our 'unhealthy' pleasures will be driven under the counter next? Sweets? Crisps? Fizzy drinks? When you give political zealots so much power, you never know quite where it will end up."[1]

If the intention is to reduce the smoking rates then it will almost certainly fail. Iceland banned tobacco displays in 2001 but smoking rates for boys have been static ever since and worse for girls. In Saskatchewan in Canada regulations quite similar to what is proposed for the UK were introduced in 2003 and, lo and behold, youth smoking rates increased at a time when they were falling elsewhere in the rest of Canada. Is there not a real danger that by making the trade in cigarettes practically illicit we will actively encourage young people to want them even more?

As ever the people who will be hit hardest by a tobacco display ban are not the big manufacturers – cigarettes will continue to sell in their millions – but ordinary people who own and use local shops. Owners of many small shops will struggle to afford the cost of the extra regulation. Product will have to be kept out of sight, difficult to manage and difficult to sell. Smaller shops may have to reduce the number of brands they can stock, which is good news for larger, rival stores. Big supermarkets, in particular, are sure to benefit at the expense of smaller shops and some local and rural stores will undoubtedly be forced to close as regular customers buy their favourite brand, along with their milk and newspapers, elsewhere. Only a bully state could impose such a policy on small retailers and their customers.

The UK has possibly the most comprehensive tobacco control policies in Europe with a ban on smoking in all enclosed public places, bans on advertising and sponsorship, annual tax increases, the raising of the minimum age for buying tobacco from 16 to 18, plus graphic health warnings. But for some that is still not enough and who better to push for further bullying of smokers than those fine examples of clean living – the nation's doctors – via their trade union, the monstrous British Medical Association. The BMA wants England to be smoke-free by 2035.[2] As well as banning the display of tobacco, it wants to outlaw cigarette vending machines and introduce plain packaging.

The BMA and other anti-smoking campaigners also wants films that portray smoking in a manner that "condones, encourages or glamourises" the habit to be reclassified for adult viewing and for anti-smoking adverts to run before they are shown. In other words, the BMA want to make films less realistic by having scenes in which people are smoking deleted, or have them reclassified as an 'adult' movie. In fact it was recently pointed out that very few top ten box office films feature anyone smoking these days. Yet again, the anti-smoking lobby is grandstanding for a cheap headline.

Anyone who, like me, lived through the Sixties and Seventies and can recall all the nonsense that surrounded the classification of Hammer Horror films, Ken Russell's *The Devils*, movies such as *The Exorcist* or racy films such as *Emmanuelle* can only laugh that people would seriously try to censor scenes featuring anyone smoking or put them out of sight of adolescents. One only has to see the amount of swearing, sexual innuendo, pelvic thrusting and violence in films of a PG category to marvel that the sight of someone smoking could result in a 15 or 12A being reclassified as an 18. According to Neil Rafferty, spokesman for the smokers' lobby Forest: "*Casablanca, All About Eve, From Here to Eternity* and *Bridge on the River Kwai* would all have to be shown after the 9.00pm watershed [on television]. And let's not forget the original cartoon version of *101 Dalmatians*, featuring that nasty tobacco user Cruella de Vil. It all starts to sound just a little bit extreme, doesn't it?"[3]

According to the anti-smoking bullies, however, seeing people smoking on film or television makes children want to smoke. Ah, the glamour of it all! So let's censor it, let's expunge it from our lives, let's make a perfectly legal habit seem unusual, taboo, abnormal even. Let's ban smoking everywhere possible so that it becomes, well, cool and rebellious! It's this sort of muddled thinking that needs to be challenged, not smoking in a handful of scenes in a small number of top box office hits. By the same logic violent gun fights and car chases would have to be edited out of films too. After all, we don't want to encourage people to shoot one another or drive dangerously fast on public roads!

Councillors from ten councils in Greater Manchester have launched a "challenging and audacious" manifesto to start a fresh campaign of anti-smoking measures to improve health. It includes proposals to refuse council grants to any local theatre that dares to stage plays in which actors smoke. This goes even further than the current smoking ban that exempts smoking on stage if "the artistic integrity of a performance makes it appropriate for a person to smoke". Other proposals include banning smoking in cars and on television. Equity, the actors' union, was suitably appalled by this artistic totalitarianism. Spokesman Martin McGrath said: "It would be ridiculous to introduce a blanket ban that doesn't take into account the artistic integrity of a performance or the circumstance. What if there was a play about someone dying of lung cancer? Would you honestly ban the protagonists of that play from portraying how smoking has (sic) given them a disease?" [4]

Aside from escapist fantasies, the power in some dramatic productions is a direct result of the film or play being based on reality. To censor this and allow only a world in which no-one smokes is a clear form of censorship that is incompatible with a free society. Teenagers do not start smoking because they see people smoke in films or on stage. They take up smoking because of direct and indirect peer pressure, because members of their family smoke, from a desire to appear grown up, or because they want to try something new (something, perhaps, that adults keep telling them not to do).

Sadly, in Britain today it's no longer enough to give consumers information about the health risks of smoking (no matter how inaccurate or exaggerated that information). It's not even enough to plaster packets of cigarettes with vivid pictures of diseased hearts and lungs. People can no longer be left to make up their own minds about the joys or evils of tobacco. Anything that could conceivably encourage us to start or even continue smoking has to be forcibly removed from the world around us.

Another idea that has the support of many politicians is plain packaging, which I understand would prohibit the use of any colour other than black and white on cigarette packs.[5] What's the thinking behind this dull, conformist view of the world? Apparently, children can identify brands by the colour of the packaging and link them with being cool. Funnily enough, this threat to cigarette packaging reminds me that for a short period in the Nineties a small company in Britain produced a brand of cigarette they called Death. If memory serves, Death cigarettes were distributed in plain black packets. Not a single bright or sexy colour in sight, yet in some circles Death cigarettes were the epitome of cool.

"Ah," the zealots will say, "it's the combination of all these restrictions that will discourage children from smoking." Wrong again. All these measures are almost certain to make cigarettes appear more alluring, more adult. The more difficult they are to come by, the more rebellious it will seem to smoke. No amount of restrictions will kill the desire for children to experiment, to show-off, to demonstrate they are beyond the control of adults. More than ever, smoking will represent a single digit finger to authority. Still don't believe me? Then ask yourself this. Despite decades of criminal convictions, despite millions of pounds being spent on educational campaigns, despite countless efforts to get us to stop, why do so many people (some of whom go on to become world leaders and respected members of the community) still choose to smoke cannabis in their teens?

The type of laws, regulations and coercion that are currently being introduced on a regular basis are often the source of the coolness not the antidote to it. Of course the real reason that many anti-tobacco bullies want to introduce more and more restrictions is not because it will stop children from smoking. No, it all comes back to denormalisation. The goal is to deliver a smoke-free Britain some time this century and denormalisation is the principal weapon that the bully state intends to employ in its desperate attempt to win the war on tobacco.

Meanwhile the obsession with health and safety (some would call it downright intrusiveness) has led to politicians and officials looking for other areas to invade, all in the name of protection. In Illinois a Democratic state legislator introduced a bill that would make texting while crossing the street a misdemeanor.[6] In Oregon a state senator dropped a proposal for a helmet law to cover all cyclists including adults, but only after he was ridiculed in the press and the blogosphere. No doubt this idea will come again. If so, why stop at helmets? What about knee and elbow pads? And why just cyclists?[7]

In Riviera Beach, Florida, the authorities have even tried to dictate how people wear their clothes. Kenneth Smith was standing on a sidewalk minding his own business when a cop noticed he wasn't dressed according to the city ordinance. His underpants were showing! In a bid to crack down on a fashion common to urban youth and hip-hop fans, Riviera Beach voters approved the new ruling in 2008. First time "exposers of undergarments in public" faced a fine of $150 and repeat offenders faced up to 30 days in jail. According to the police officer, Smith's brown and white plaid shorts "were so low that it exposed his blue and white boxer shorts approximately two inches below his waist". Following another case of a 17-year-old who spent a night in jail for having his underwear showing, a Florida judge said that Riviera Beach's "saggy pants" law was unconstitutional.[8]

This is not the nanny state at work. It has nothing to do with 'protection', although the fashion victims involved may look back at photos in later years and cringe, like I do when I see myself in my Seventies' tank tops and brothel creepers. This is plain and simple prurience. Riviera beach voters found this fashion unsightly and offensive and chose to ban it, but I consider that action to be just as daft as wearing one's trousers at half mast or with your underpants showing.

Councils often use legislation beyond its original intentions. An attempt by government in Scotland to reduce the amount of noise pollution that we all face has all the makings of a well-intentioned act that can spiral into unnecessary intervention. As if councils up and down the land don't have enough on their plate, they are now going to be working to produce 'noise-maps' that show which urban areas have the greatest noise, and then they are going to plan to reduce the noise, targeting traffic. For instance, a total of 19 areas across Edinburgh are set to be designated "noise management areas" as part of a new Scottish Government drive to tackle excessive noise.

One would hope that the campaign would start and end with the construction or maintenance by councils of their local roads so that low-noise surfacing is used wherever possible and shrubbery and landscaping is used for effective noise screening. Instead some of restrictions being considered include "banning certain types of vehicles, limiting the time of day vehicles have access to a road and varying speed limits". According to the local *Evening News* "It is thought planners will also be urged to insist on rigorous noise controls for new developments".[9]

We all know one sources of noise pollution: speed humps. Cars slow down, change gear, thump over the bump, and then accelerate towards the next one, doing untold long-term damage to their vehicle. Will the council rip up these "traffic calming measures" that cause more trouble than they're worth? I doubt it. Once again the car, that great symbol of individual freedom, is the prime target and those ever changing speed restrictions are a valuable weapon to target the driver. What vehicles will be banned and how will it be policed? Can we expect more council inspectors and faux-police to be employed by the council? The campaign may appear well-intentioned but with politicians at the helm even the most attractive-sounding policy can become a bullies' charter.

The car is a popular target for today's politicians. Daytime running lights, the enforcement by law of all cars having their headlights on whenever the ignition is turned on, is to be introduced across the European Union over the next few years. The idea is that they help drivers see other vehicles on the roads but the evidence suggests that it becomes far harder to distinguish between cars and motorcycles, which can be lost in a constellation of bright lights or can be masked by the dazzle. The European Commission argues that road casualties will be reduced by introducing dedicated high visibility daytime running lights (DRL) on all new cars and commercial vehicles from February 2011, but the Motorcycle Action Group (MAG) says that compulsory daytime use is no substitute for driver awareness and expects this new law to increase the risk of death through fatal accidents to motorcyclists.[10] Under pressure from MAG and others the EU climbed down from applying the law to all cars, but phasing it in through laws on new cars does not change the outcome, it only delays it.

In the field of food there is also a hunger for more control. After trans fats, salt is the next target of the bellicose bullies and, surprise, surprise, New York is again at the forefront. "In many ways, high blood pressure is a forgotten killer. It's the leading cause of early death in New York City and nationally," said the city's health commissioner Dr Thomas Frieden following the publication of a study by his department linking salt intake to chronic diseases.

The Journal of the American Medical Association published an article that claimed that "Processed and restaurant foods account for 77 per cent of salt consumption, so it is nearly impossible for consumers to greatly reduce their own salt intake." Intervention thus justified, the article suggested marketing restrictions on certain types of food, price subsidies for government-favoured foods, planning restrictions on restaurants that serve 'bad foods' or the use of taxation to curb their consumption. "The modern food supply is tainted – it is too salty, too sugary, and too rich in calories, and there is simply too much of such food easily available," the authors argued. They went on: "Food safety for the 21st century should be reframed ... public health systems must reduce the contribution of food to the epidemics of obesity and chronic disease." If that isn't the landing craft arriving on the shore, making the first assault to establish the beachhead for further incursion, I don't know what is.

There remains one problem with all of this. Salt has not actually been conclusively proven to contribute to either high blood pressure or heart disease. It is an essential part of our daily diet. Too much or too little can be bad for you but moderating its use is something that the majority of people can do by themselves. Indeed New York's own study found that only a minority, 26 per cent, of residents was taking 'too much' salt. In other words 74 per cent were doing just fine. The target of New York's Department of Health and Mental Hygiene will initially be restaurants, because that's where the health police have jurisdiction, but even in such a tourist-orientated city as New York only 25 per cent of meals are consumed outside the home so to be effective the campaigners are also lobbying for federal laws covering manufacturers of processed foods and have given evidence at a Food and Drug Administration hearing.[11]

Closer to home the creation of an anti-salt mentality has resulted in Marmite being banned from a Welsh school.[12] Now you either love it or hate it, but banning Marmite is hardly going to reduce the likelihood of hypertension. Children attending Pontrhydfendigaid primary school in west Wales found that it was removed from their breakfast club and that of the 50 other primary schools in Ceredigion. One mother protested saying, "It is the nanny state going too far. Generations of my family have grown up on Marmite. If children like the taste of Marmite and it encourages them to eat breakfast then that is a good thing." Amen to that, I say.

Ceredigion Council tried to blame guidance received from the Welsh Assembly, which funds the breakfast clubs, but its spokesman retorted: "We have not mentioned Marmite in our guidance. In terms of toppings for toast we indicate these are optional and where required a low fat polyunsaturated spread should be used and similarly a reduced sugar jam. Anything served must be healthy and nutritionally balanced. Marmite is not included on the list of items as it does include a high level of salt." One can only surmise that some overzealous apparatchik took the 'reduced sugar content' as a green light for 'reduced salt content' and banned Marmite, but a typical child's serving of Marmite of 2.0g, provides 0.25g of salt, only six per cent of a child's recommended daily intake.

It gets even sillier. New EU regulations have banned the consumption of cakes and confectionary entered at country fairs and agricultural shows immediately after baking competitions. The cake cannot be consumed, it has to be destroyed to protect us from food poisoning. Under the new EU rules the judges of bakery sections are only permitted to taste the traditional favourites such as scones or soda bread. Once the judging is over the entries must be disposed of immediately. The directive has already been made law in Scotland (now there's a surprise!). In Ireland the chairman of Mayo County Council, Joe Mellett, said the new rules would be the "death knell" for the Irish agricultural show. "When you see things like this it's no wonder the people voted no to the Lisbon Treaty. This will be the end of the traditional baking competition at local shows across the country, therefore impacting on local revenue. It's just ridiculous."[13]

Europe is not alone in having daft laws about food. Los Angeles is already restricting new fast food restaurants and New York is thinking of doing the same thing. Proponents of this policy argue that fast food 'causes' obesity and that leads to medical expenses that the poor can't afford and taxpayers have to pay for, making it a public not a private issue. Commentator Duane Lester observed: "Instead of seeing the welfare state as a problem, they see freedom of choice. Rather than eliminate the free health care, they eliminate freedom. Rather than move away from socialism, they move away from liberty."

The desire to control our behaviour even more is not limited to socialists or European bureacrats. There is a strong paternalist strain in the Conservative party and it was the Tories who gave us the Criminal Justice Act which makes it illegal to have an outdoor party with live music without a licence. David Cameron has always been adamant that a new version of the married couples' allowance that Labour scrapped will be introduced, covering civil partnerships too. His idea is to support parents in the belief, supported by a substantial body of evidence, that married parents provide a more secure foundation for raising families.[14]

Cameron's proposals would ensure that swanky fat cats who just happen to be married but are childless would receive a state benefit whilst poor unmarried parents would not. Single mothers, the majority of whom have been deserted by their husbands, would gain nothing under a marriage benefit or tax break. Shadow chancellor George Osborne apparently disagrees with Cameron, believing that the state should not tell people how to live their lives. Instead he believes all parents should be given encouragement and support.

Watch this space to see what the Conservatives actually do if given the chance, but alarm bells are already ringing. What exactly was Tory shadow education secretary Michael Gove doing when he said: "I believe we need to ask tough questions about the instant-hit hedonism celebrated by the modern men's magazines targeted at younger males. Titles such as *Nuts* and *Zoo* paint a picture of women as permanently, lasciviously, uncomplicatedly available. The images they use and project reinforce a very narrow conception of beauty and a shallow approach towards women. They celebrate thrill-seeking and instant gratification without ever allowing any thought of responsibility towards others, or commitment, to intrude."

Excuse me, but does Michael Gove really know what he is talking about? Does he buy *Nuts* and *Zoo* or is he above all that and only goes for the more upmarket lads mag like *FHM*? Probably none of these because like me, he is undoubtedly a *Spectator* reader as he occasionally writes for it. Well, my sons have read lads mags from time to time – they've even had an *FHM* calendar! They are perfectly normal blokes in their twenties who don't believe that women are "permanently, lasciviously, uncomplicatedly available" because of the occasional tits out, legs-akimbo photograph you find in some magazines, any more than they think women are congenitally frumpy, healed-up spinsters because they were taught by the odd man-hater at school.

As a former culture spokesman Michael Gove must know that scantily clad women have been featured in photographs since the first negatives were developed. Some are now priceless collectors' items. Should they be reserved for luvvies and arts buffs to look at in the privacy of their studies, or is the modern proletonian Tory party going to concede that blue collar boys can look at the modern equivalent too, after completing an oil change of their secondhand Ford Focus? The weeklies *Nuts*, *Zoo*, and the monthlies *FHM*, *Loaded* and *Maxim* sell 653,000 copies between them, far more than the 75,000 who read *The Spectator* each week. That's quite a lot of readers to upset.

Is Gove actually proposing to do something about these magazines? Would a future Tory government regulate the content or sale of such magazines? Are they going to be put below the counter alongside cigarettes? Yes? No? Well, if nothing's going to happen why mention it? He told the Institute for Public Policy Research (Tony Blair's favourite think tank, remember): "Helping adults commit and stay committed not only opens the door to a depth of emotional enrichment which a series of shallow and hedonistic encounters can never generate, it also provides the best possible start in life for children." Well, I don't disagree with that, but at the same time what's wrong with people enjoying some hedonism on the way to finding the right partner? That's what probably most of us do, even if it's to find out that hedonism is not all it's cracked up to be and we may not care for it after all!

Jonathan Shephard, chief executive of the Periodical Publishers Association, said: "Michael Gove raises deep and complex social issues which reach far wider than simply reading a magazine. To try to create an unsubstantiated causal link between these issues and men's magazines is unrealistic." Damn right it is. Personally I think Shephard was a tad diplomatic in his choice of words. And just in case Gove thought all his moody nudging was going to win him and his party some sympathy, Jane Ahrends, spokeswoman for Gingerbread (the one parent families group), said: "The shadow secretary's declared commitment to families is welcome but it is difficult to see how family life and responsible parenting would be strengthened by work requirements for single parents of young children, as proposed by the party, or how child poverty would be addressed by tax breaks for married parents only."[15]

As you can see, one person's tax break is another person's nannying. Ahrends went on: "Most single parents have been married and expected their families to stay intact … separation is not a path most chose lightly." The Tory party can't resist revealing its own 'nanny' default position if it thinks there may be a vote in it, only these days it is more interested in imparting a mood to the electorate than committing to action, something that – for the party that brought us compulsory seat belts – we should be relieved about.

Notes:
1.  Dr Eamonn Butler, *The Free Society*
2.  *The Independent*, 7 July 2008
3.  Neil Rafferty, *The Free Society*
4.  *The Independent*, 25 July 2008
5.  *Daily Telegraph*, 31 May 2008
6.  Guerilla News Network, 23 August 2008
7.  DemocratHerald.Com, Albany, Oregon 5 August 2008
8.  Sphere.com 3 September 2008
9   *Evening News*, Edinburgh, 25 July 2008
10. mag.qtweb.co.uk, 25 September 2008
11. *New York Sun*, 29 September 2008, and saltinstitute.org

12. *Daily Mail*, 10 October 2008. The food industry's guideline daily amount of salt for a child aged five to ten is 4.0g

13. Sphere.com 27 August 2008

14. *The Times*, 5 August 2008. Almost half of cohabiting couples split up before their child's fifth birthday, compared with 8.33% of married people

15. *Press and Journal*, 5 August 2008

# Chapter Nine

# BULLIES ARE LOSERS

*"Always vote for principle, though you may vote alone,
and you may cherish the sweetest reflection
that your vote is never lost."*

\- JOHN QUINCY ADAMS

There are bullies in every walk of life but if you think back to the school playground I wager that the bullies often lost in the end. Not immediately, perhaps not even at school, but eventually they were found out, defeated and punished. There are always opportunities to fight back and when the persecuted get together the bully often backs down and moves out.

Playground bullies will always enjoy some success but we all know that bullies are essentially losers and lifestyle bullies are no different. What goes around comes around and bullies are on the losing side are more often than you might think. (No political system based on the suppression of individual liberty lasts forever. Ask the inhabitants of the former Soviet Union.)

Nevertheless we have to recognise that as things stand we are standing at the crossroads and we have a choice. Do we allow ourselves to be frogmarched down the road towards a bully state, a false Utopia where every decision is made for us and we are monitored every step of the way "in our own best interests'; or do we take control of our lives and choose the path towards a more tolerant, less regulated world?

In the post war age we have seen the conjunction of four phenomena: the mutation of public health away from the fight against communicable diseases that required a community-based response towards direct intrusion into our lifestyles; the growth of health and safety which is designed to create a risk-free environment but which makes us less aware of danger and less able to cope without the 'support' of the state; the growth of socialised healthcare that gives the state a large vested interest in not just our diets but also our recreational pleasures; and the death of socialism followed by its subsequent resurrection as a lifestyle commissar that harnesses public health, health and safety and socialised healthcare to its own ends.

There's an irony here because one might have thought that the overthrow of communism in Eastern Europe would have given people in Western Europe the strength to resist those forces that are conspiring to bully us into behaving in a manner approved by the state. Sadly it is not that simple. I agree with Professor James Buchanan, the Nobel laureate responsible for the school of public choice theory, who argues that socialists, having lost the philosophical and economic argument, have regrouped and are now using lifestyle control as a means to reassert the will of the collective over the individual.

Socialists of varying hues have forsaken their jackboots, their boiler suits and their AK47s and are instead using surveillance, regulation, guidance, inspection, by-laws, and local summary justice as weapons to subjugate us. These neo-socialists may not want to nationalise the top 100 British companies but by banning smoking in all enclosed public places the British pub is no longer the licensed but private jurisdiction of the landlord. Likewise the proposal to ban the display of tobacco in shops is an extraordinary intrusion by the state into the lives of ordinary people.

Lifestyle socialism is not restricted to those on the left of the political spectrum. It has its attractions for those on the right as well. The Conservative party has always had an unhealthy number of paternalists. For many years in the post war era many Tories rejected the idea that there was a philosophical battle to be fought between socialism and capitalism. They naively believed that they merely had to manage the welfare system more efficiently (or more compassionately) than their socialist opponents. As a result an entire generation of Britons witnessed the ratchet effect whereby the Labour governments of Attlee and Wilson progressively created a socialist state that successive Conservative governments did nothing to reverse. It was only when Margaret Thatcher came to power in 1979 that the ratchet was actively reversed.

There are plenty of Conservatives who still have a soft spot for the nanny state, often because they harbour their own patrician hobbyhorse. Like their socialist counterparts they cannot abide the idea that we might make the 'wrong' choices or that those choices, like choosing to shop in a superstore rather than the local village shop, may shape society in a manner that is different from their own particular idyll. Some of these traits were suppressed during Margaret Thatcher's reign. Now however they are back in vogue as senior Conservatives talk openly of "nudging" people in the 'right' direction. As political commentator Simon Heffer argued in the *Daily Telegraph*, there may be a Conservative election victory in 2010 but there's unlikely to be a Conservative government. If the bully state that has developed under Tony Blair and Gordon Brown is to be reversed I do hope Heffer is wrong.

I live in hope that the Liberal Democrats will rediscover their roots in the old Liberal party of free trade and personal responsibility but that tradition was ditched by David Lloyd George and the party has never really recovered. "Why vote for moderate Liberal socialism when you can get the real thing with Labour?" was the obvious deduction made by the British electorate during the twentieth century. Having joined forces with the short-lived Social

Democrats in the Eighties, the Liberal party remains on life support. While there may be the occasional twitch, a finger might rise and in between drools the mouth mutters words such as "freedom" and "individual responsibility", all attempts to make the Liberal Democrats live up to their name fail. (How liberal are the Liberal Democrats? Do I really need to answer that rhetorical question?)

As for the Scottish and Welsh nationalists, there's no hope there. Their brand of socialism not only leaves them well to the left of New Labour, but such is the nature of devolution any opportunity to justify the existence of the Scottish Parliament and Welsh Assembly and pass new laws is grasped with barely suppressed glee. With the Scottish Nationalists in power in the Scottish Parliament, the party's bully state tendencies are self-evident. No-one should be surprised. It was, after all, from the ranks of the SNP that a smoking ban was first mooted in the shape of a private bill during the previous Scottish parliament, and the most enthusiastic supporters of the Scottish Labour government's subsequent bill were the Nationalists themselves.

Today alcohol has joined tobacco in the SNP's sights and Labour is playing catch-up yet again. Expect more examples of intrusive government the longer the Nationalists remain in charge if only because, having waited so long to achieve power in Scotland, this is their chance to put their own stamp (and I use the word advisedly) on the nation. As for the Greens, wherever they are elected you can be sure they will support almost any interventionist policies, especially regulations designed to 'protect' us from using the wrong light bulbs, installing the wrong showers, or using a powerful motor vehicle.

Nor is neo-socialism reserved for political parties. It pervades many if not all government institutions especially at local level where the jobsworth mentality has always flourished with officials applying new laws with as strict an interpretation as possible. Quangos that, in my experience as a politician, are to all intents and purposes unaccountable, are especially insidious and influential. They exert a power over our lives that is difficult to identify, never mind challenge. Health boards and health authorities, or groups set up to promote and police policies on our health, our driving, or our general behaviour, litter the political landscape as if they have some divine right to tell us what is in our best interests. They lobby political parties, spending vast sums of taxpayers' money in the process, and then expect politicians and governments to accept their recommendations without question. This self-serving elite continues to grow in scale and reach despite perennial promises by politicians to prune them back.

Then there are those 'fake' charities and campaign groups that have wilfully taken the state's silver so they are no longer independent of government but are its storm troopers, propagandists and fellow travellers. Health charities are especially prone to this behaviour.

The result is political parties that have willingly adopted positions where they can justify greater intervention in our lifestyle; agencies that claim to be at arms length from government, yet are working hand in hand with the state to control our behaviour, at further cost to the taxpayers who are paying their wages; and groups that claim to be independent but have become tools of the government. Together they are helping to create the modern bully state.

It is easy for the public to believe that the avalanche of rules and regulations, be it at European, national or local level, is irreversible. But I've got news for you. It can. But first we have to win the battle of ideas. Just as socialism, or the 57 varieties various of communism it mutated into, was defeated by a robust and principled adherence to philosophical argument, so too can we challenge the lifestyle socialists who want to control every aspect of our lives.

Whatever you think of Margaret Thatcher and Ronald Reagan, I believe it was their leadership and the support they got from other NATO leaders that ensured that communism crumbled. The same success could be achieved in tackling the bully state with a more united front but this is exactly where the defenders of individual rights and personal liberty fall down. Our very individuality means that we are a disunited bunch and this weakness is regularly exploited.

Tobacco has been picked on for years and the food and drink manufacturers kept quiet believing that any association with the 'evil weed' tainted them. In recent years this has led to the drinks industry declining to share a platform with Big Tobacco or support the consumers of tobacco, even though most smokers are no strangers to alcohol.

The argument is sometimes made that there are no people marching along the streets protesting against the nanny state, let alone the bully state. Maybe it's because people work around these minor infringements of their liberties. People grumble but the vast majority are law abiding and we don't want to make a fuss. One day, possibly soon, people will realise that they have lost a huge number of small freedoms that, years earlier, they took for granted.

I firmly believe that few people in Britain support an intolerant, highly regulated society. Opinion polls carried out by the Office for National Statistics prior to the introduction of the smoking ban in England and Wales made it clear that the public wanted smoke-free to become the norm in most public places, but when offered a choice of outcomes (rather than a straight ban or no ban) 70 per cent consistently vetoed the idea of a blanket ban on smoking in pubs and clubs. By supporting a lighter touch the British public showed a greater tolerance for pluralism and tolerance than our politicians have delivered. Likewise the current wave of tobacco controls is not driven by public demand, whatever politicians might say. So-called 'public consultations' are nothing of the sort. They are clearly manipulated by government using taxpayers' money to generate a result that supports official government policy. It's quite scandalous and is symptomatic of the bully state

Supporters defend the nanny state by portraying critics as laissez faire libertarians who want the government to do nothing. This misses the point. The argument is not about whether or not to have speed restrictions on roads or drink driving limits but what the appropriate speed for a certain road is and the amount of alcohol that should be allowed in a driver's blood. It comes back to the argument that the poison is in the dose, not the substance. The bully state now seeks to ban the substance rather than limit the dose, be it trans fat or tobacco smoke. No accommodation can be made, even though all the evidence suggests that it's the dose that matters. The result is that whereas governments in the past wanted to improve our lives by delivering greater provision for us but left us to make the choices, modern day government tries to improve our lives by controlling our lifestyle through eliminating the choices they don't want us to make.

The happy medium is to give people a choice whilst protecting us from those who have no respect for other people's choices. I have as little sympathy for the person who says "I'll smoke wherever I want" as I have for the person who says "I don't like being exposed to tobacco smoke so I want every pub and club in the country to be smoke free". One is just as bad as the other. The answer, in a tolerant, civilised society, is to find a solution that can accommodate everyone, within reason.

The traditional 'British' way, tolerating other peoples' habits and eccentricities, has become a thing of the past. We are witnessing the end of tolerance and it is not a pretty sight. Such is the shift from the nanny to the bully state that many might welcome the return of nanny, but it's too late for that. To win the argument we have to take on and defeat the whole concept of nannying because bullying is simply a more extreme version of the same dogma. Just as totalitarian communism arose from the failure of democratic socialism to deliver its promised fruits, so the bully state emerged from the failure of the nanny state to rid the world of smoking and other 'anti-social' habits. Communism was defeated by challenging the central arguments of socialist planning and the bully state will be defeated by challenging the arguments that justify a nanny state.

Politicians do not have a right to tell us how to live, beyond preventing us from infringing other peoples' liberties.

The degree to which the state can intervene in people's lives is illustrated by the cigar club I was a member of in Scotland. It met for three years in a public house called Canon's Gait just 500 yards from the Edinburgh Parliament. The bar had a small basement function room that was ideal for such occasions with no staff involved until the next morning when they would clear up after the meeting. There was no conceivable health risk to any member of staff. Cigar tastings took place, often with a Caribbean rum or a Brazilian spirit to establish which stogies went best with which liquor. No one attended who was not a consenting adult. Nevertheless, after the smoking ban was introduced it was impossible for this congenial and civilised club to continue. Venues that would allow 20 or so people to meet and smoke cigars indoors – a necessary aspect of Scotland's cold and unpredictable climate – no longer exist in Scotland, other than peoples' private houses.

In Britain today there seems to be no limit to the level of nannying and bullying. Toleration of 'errant' behaviour must not only to be discouraged but people's lifestyles must be outlawed and criminalised. Having read this you may still think that the smoking ban is a good thing but consider another example of the nanny/bully state. In September 2006 a green quango that receives over one million pounds a year of public money announced we would all benefit if people stopped buying kilts and hired them instead. Yes, kilts! According to the *Daily Record*, "Green activists funded by taxpayers' money were branded tartan barmy yesterday after they told Scots to save the world by sharing kilts. Bosses at campaigning outfit the Scottish Waste Awareness Group claim Scots who buy their own Highland dress are harming the planet."

Some people seldom wear a kilt so hiring one for special occasions makes sense. Others will wear it far more often. They may even pass it on to a family member so the investment is well worth the money. But no, SWAG thought that buying a kilt should be discouraged. One can only speculate about how far this plan would be taken and how it would be enforced. Would a shopkeeper be fined for selling kilts? Would the wearer have to carry proof of hire in his sporran? Absurd, yes, but no more daft than the idea of a smoking permit which I addressed in an earlier chapter. Surely people can decide for themselves what's best for them? To paraphrase an old advertising slogan, a kilt is for life, not just for weddings.

Another approach adopted by the state is to encourage 'good' behaviour rather than penalising 'bad' behaviour. This includes tax cuts or subsidies instead of a fine or punitive levy. Personally I see this as little better because it still concedes the principle that politicians know better than us. We are still being controlled, directed and, yes, nudged by the state. Facilitating good behaviour may sound admirable but it still requires someone to decide what is good or bad for us and with it the development of responsibility that develops from a growing self-awareness of the consequences of one's actions.

If there's one thing I can predict with absolute certainty it is that in the short time between the completion of this book's manuscript and its publication there will have been more instances of government data being lost, more research telling us that foods previously thought to be life-enhancing are in fact dangerous, and further calls by politicians and their parasitic lobbyists for even more rules and regulations because the vast library of statutes is still not enough.

Faced with such an irresistible tsunami of legislation, what can be done? How can we defend those freedoms we still have, let alone roll back the bully state? We must start by asking politicians hard questions about what they have done in the past and will do in the future to defend individual liberties. (Be specific and give examples that they have to take a position on. Politicians hate detailed questions and prefer not to be pinned down on specific issues.)

Demand of our leaders and their political opponents what they will do to roll back the bully state, not just the meddlesome bans and restrictions on alcohol, food and tobacco but more generally in the areas of public health and health and safety. If politicians want us to behave like adults they should stop treating us like children and allow us to make our own mistakes so we can learn from them and move on.

The United States has a Bill of Rights and a Constitution that can only be amended with great difficulty and is defended jealously by the Supreme Court. Britain's defence of individual liberty relies upon our parliamentary democracy debating proposed legislation and holding the government to account, but this seems to be a thing of the past. The amount of time given to scrutinising new legislation is laughable. We may have the European Convention on Human Rights but its very broad principles can be widely interpreted by courts that are not accountable to the British people.

There is however hope. Hope that pernicious prohibitions can be amended or repealed. It won't happen overnight. The surveillance state, the introduction of smoking bans and restrictions on our eating and drinking habits have not happened overnight and it will take time to reverse the trend, but it is possible. The response has to be strategic and tactical, using international examples of how more tolerance is beneficial, challenging false claims and convincing politicians, or change merchants, that change will benefit them too – a better relationship, perhaps, between politicians and the people. We cannot return to the old status quo, but we can try to create a new, more favourable consensus.

There is hope that we might amend the smoking ban to allow, for example, separate smoking rooms. The prospect of an amendment may seem unlikely now but it is certainly not impossible. The demise of the British pub, for which a significant amount of blame can be placed on the smoking ban despite what some trade apologists say, has reached such proportions that people are at last willing to speak out in favour of relaxing the ban.

Launched in June 2009 Forest's Save Our Pubs & Clubs: Amend The Smoking Ban campaign has the support of MPs from the three main parties. Greg Knight, Conservative MP for East Yorkshire, told journalists: "I fully support this campaign. Britain's pubs and clubs are at the heart of every local community and the UK approach of banning indoor smoking everywhere is damaging the viability of many licensed premises where people wish to smoke. Pub landlords and club committees know best what their customers want and they should be allowed to provide smoking rooms if there is a demand."

The campaign also has the support of Eamonn Butler, director of the Adam Smith Institute and the author of *The Rotten State of Britain*. Butler spoke for many non-smokers when he said: "I'm not a smoker, but I'm appalled to see the damage that the smoking ban has already done to our pubs and clubs. The politicians aren't just trying to control people's lives, they're ruining people's businesses as well. If consenting adults want to smoke in a designated smoking room, why shouldn't they?"

It won't be easy to amend the ban because any concession, no matter how small, will be fiercely resisted. For the bully state, compromise is not an option. The good news is that other European countries, including Germany and Spain, have adopted a more tolerant, practical approach. A concerted campaign, supported by smokers and tolerant non-smokers, including those whose drinking and eating habits are now under attack, could make a difference.

Even within the NHS there are people who are fighting to prevent further controls, like restrictions on operations for people who smoke, drink or are obese. Interviewed by the *Daily Telegraph*, Andrew Dillon, chief executive of the National Institute for Health and Clinical Excellence (NICE), said that personal lifestyle choice should not be used as a reason to deny people treatment on the NHS. According to Dillon: "The only circumstances in which we say the way people behave individually should be taken into account is if that behaviour has the effect of directly reducing the effectiveness of the treatment. Simply because you have a lifestyle is not a reason for refusing a treatment. If that was the case any of us who go skiing would be told if you get a broken leg don't expect us to fix it.

"It is a lifestyle choice if you ski. I like to ski. I go out and I know there is a much greater risk of serious injury than if I didn't go skiing or if I went walking in the Lake District or lay on a beach instead and no-one says to me because of that lifestyle choice the NHS will treat you differently. I think we have to be extremely careful about saying that the way people live their lives is a factor in decision making and NICE has said it isn't, except where continuing with a particular pattern of lifestyle renders the treatment ineffective." [1]

Thank goodness for the clear thinking logic of Andrew Dillon. As long as people are prepared speak out, the bully state can be exposed, ridiculed and defeated.

It pays to challenge the authorities and when voters have a say the bullies are often the losers. The 2008 general election in New Zealand offers hope to those who want to beat the bully state rather than merely defy its laws. The Labour government had planned to change the allowable flow rates for showers in new homes exceeding 150 square metres to six litres a minute, a rate that plumbers likened to a dribble. The issue became a cause célèbre even though the new regulation only applied to new homes of a certain size and was not retrospective to any existing homes. Nick Smith MP, building and construction spokesman for the opposition National party, said: "Labour's nanny state is out of control. They tell us how to live our lives by doing things like dictating what can and can't be sold in school tuck-shops and what light bulbs we can use, and now how much water we can use when showering.

"There is no rhyme or reason to these regulations. One's house size should not affect how much water you can use in your shower. It is illogical to put restrictions on shower flows when no restrictions are put on bathing which uses significantly more energy. These regulations apply even if you're not connected to the national grid or town water supply. These regulations are a misguided attempt at efficiency. What they really are is about using less. We don't have to be so green that we can't be clean. People should be free to use as much water as they like when showering, provided they don't expect others to pay for their profligacy. User pays is a far better approach than nanny state." 2

The public seemed to agree, no doubt feeling that once introduced the law could be easily refreshed to include everyone else so the change had to be resisted. With more than 75 per cent of new homes exceeding 150 square metres the next logical step would have been to include all homes and then any new appliances. Another example of daft regulations in New Zealand was a kindergarten that had trouble with its gate latch. The local council's building code required a gate latch to be low enough to allow disabled access but the education regulations (and common sense) required the latch to be high enough to prevent children escaping onto the road.

So hot did these nanny state debates become that the Labour government withdrew its shower flow proposal but it was too late. Labour was given an early bath in the general election. The prevalence of nanny state issues in the election contributed to the feeling that government was too arrogant and too big for everyone's good.

History has many examples of restrictive practices being defeated. Andrew J Volstead was one of the most influential Americans of the 20th century and yet his name is little remembered now, even in the USA. His name was given to the 18th Amendment to the American Constitution, the Volstead Act, passed in January 1919 but known and understood now as the dawn of prohibition. The theory was simple enough: ban the sale and distribution of alcohol and this would cause the nation's crime rate to drop and the people's health to improve as less alcohol was drunk. People would commit less crime, they would have fewer illnesses, and the world would be a better, more sober, place. It didn't quite work like that. America's thirst for booze increased rather than diminished with practically every back office, cellar and attic that could be converted into an illicit speakeasy. By 1925 there were 100,000 speakeasies in New York alone.

Crime became rife as previously legal jobs such as bartenders were outlawed and even having a celebratory drink became illegal. Murders increased by nearly 80 per cent, the general crime rate nearly doubled and federal convicts increased by a staggering 561 per cent. Not only did the crime rate worsen, it became organised with bootleggers developing huge businesses that required teams of people to work outside the law and to defend their market share with death and violence or the threat of either. In one year alone, Chicago suffered more than 400 gangster-related murders.

Meanwhile the number of deaths from alcoholism increased, the arrests for drunkenness grew (by 41 per cent) and the number of drink-driving offences mushroomed (by 81 per cent). To conceal their illicit alcohol Americans switched from beer to spirits, consuming more potent drinks and becoming drunker by drinking less, often with fatal results. Without legally enforceable standards, deaths from poisoned liquor rose from 1,064 in 1920 to 4,154 in 1925.

Today in Britain we have our own prohibitionists although they don't like to admit it. They don't (or rather won't) go that far – not yet anyway. For the moment they are satisfied introducing more and more restrictions rather than ushering in an outright ban, but prohibition will one day become the 'next logical step', just as the prohibition of smoking is the ultimate goal behind every measure that is taken to denormalise smoking. The theory is simple enough. Make booze more expensive and harder to come by and the nation's crime rate will drop and the people's health will improve as less alcohol is drunk. And yet we only have to look across the channel to France and Spain where drink is far cheaper and we will find more sober, law-abiding and healthier societies.

Today's prohibitionists in the Labour and SNP governments in Westminster and Holyrood don't have the moral courage of their predecessors to call for prohibition. Instead they would rather bully us into submission. The result? Pubs will close, people will lose their jobs, there will be more smuggling, more disregard for the law and its agencies – and the health of the nation will be no better.

But bullies are losers and we should take heart from the story of prohibition in America. Seventy-six years ago on 5 December 1933 the 21st Amendment was ratified and America's failed experiment ended. Corks popped across the country as the nation raised a glass to prohibition's demise. Prohibition can be defeated, common sense can prevail. We need to change our cultural attitudes to drink and drunkenness, not our laws or our taxes. We need our politicians to sober up and kick their dependency on bullying us for our own good.

Ultimately, if politicians and their parties cannot be trusted to put nanny into a retirement home and call a halt to the mindless bullying that they initiated, then the response has to come from outside parliament. The answer is for those of us who feel threatened, coerced or bullied by the state to coalesce and campaign together rather than apart. Bullies win when they pick people off individually but when the persecuted join together bullies can be defeated.

If this book serves no other purpose, I hope it will encourage individuals to collectively fight for the right to live your life as you see fit without the overbearing weight of the bully state making every decision for you. Freedom of choice is a right that the people of Britain have earned. Don't give up that right without a fight.

Notes:
1. *Daily Telegraph*, 26 July 2004.
2. *New Zealand Herald*, 10 October 2008

Previously there were no controls on shower flow rates and households were free to install showerheads with flows ranging from 5 litres/minute to 24 litres/minute (some are as high as 35 litres/minute). The average is 13 litres/minute.